Retire
PLAY AND
PURPOSE

How to have an amazing time going forward

Ed Zinkiewicz

Retire to Play and Purpose: How to have an amazing time going forward

ISBN (Perfectbound): 978-0-9886622-2-3
ISBN (e-Book): 978-0-9886622-3-0

Cover design and interior layout by Bookcovers.com

Medical Disclaimer

The content in this book and on the related website is for informational purposes only. It is not intended to replace professional medical advice or care from physicians or trained medical professionals. If experiencing symptoms or health problems, seek the advice of your healthcare providers.

Neither Retirement-U, Inc. nor the author provides medical treatment, medical care, or medical advice. No information conveyed by using this book and related website is meant to take the place of your physician or healthcare provider.

You must seek the opinion of a physician for treatment or diagnoses of any medical problem. Do not rely on Retirement-U, Inc. or its products for medical care or medical decision making. Never delay in seeking medical advice or attention because of something you have read in a Retirement-U, Inc. book or on Retirement-U, Inc. website.

IF YOU THINK YOU HAVE A MEDICAL EMERGENCY, CALL YOUR DOCTOR AND 911 IMMEDIATELY!

Table of Contents

For You and Footnotes

A website has been created for this book. You can find it at:

www.retireto.info/goforward/bookresources/

In general, the site has two parts:

For You: This part contains additional material you will find helpful on your road to play and purpose. Most chapters have references at the end that explain material on the site relevant to the chapter. On the website, items are noted by chapter in the For You section.

Footnotes: All of the footnotes from this book are also on the webpage, "bookresources," which is listed above. Some of the footnotes contain web links, which are active there. Just click on them and go directly to the referenced page. In the print version of this book all the web links are shortened. They are limited to their simple home page URL, which makes them easier to type into your browser.

For other resources to help you make your retirement the best of your life, go to retire-to.com.

Bonuses

You may have purchased this book at a brick and mortar or an online bookstore. As a result, you may not have known about the bonuses available to you for purchasing the book.

Don't miss out on these freebies. Just send an email to **purpose@retire-to.com,** tell me where you bought the book, if you got this book as a gift, and whether you have a paper or electronic version. And we'll do the rest.

We'll send you

1) **ReFirement Party Guide:** Take the exciting leap into retirement with a party that not only celebrates what you've done but also what you will do.

2) **ReFirement Invitations:** You'll have two different versions to choose from, ready to print and send to your friends to help celebrate.

   Dr. Jim Gambone at ReFirement, Inc. has supplied these resources to help you leap into retirement with a sendoff that matters.

3) **100 Benefits of Being Retired:** Our friend Joel Helfer, founder of Strategic Seniors, will kick-start your retirement with a set of great things to look forward to.

Introduction

Some retirement surprises don't show up the day you retire. One in particular may take a little while. Retirement has to sink in a bit. For my wife, Crys, the surprise took almost two years. For our friend Gail it took a summer. For Terry it was a general realization. But it did happen. Eventually these people turned around and began to wonder.

- Crys, for example, wondered whether life had no further meaning. The paycheck was a very important symbol for her. Not having one meant that the worth she had in her career had disappeared as well. Your worth as a human being does not fluctuate with employment opportunities. But it sure feels like a loss to some people when the symbols of being employed disappear. Crys began to ask questions: What will I do if not the work I left behind? What about all the skill I have acquired—is it just valueless?

Crys' job had been personally rewarding—highly stressful too, but satisfying. Watching the paycheck vanish was like watching the cowboy ride off, taking the sunset with him! "Hold on there, pardner. Where ya goin' with my sunset?" She did not expect that to disappear!

- Our friend Gail, on the other hand, said, "I sat in my perfectly clean living room and cried." When she retired, she finally could devote her newfound time to finishing all those chores around the house she never had time to manage while employed. But once that series of goals had been met, she felt lost. She had no plan and no sense of what else to look forward to.

- Terry missed driving the ship. With a touch of annoyance in his voice, he talked of all the years it took to work his way up the corporate ladder, only to find that he missed a key element of his former executive position. It surprised him. "I had just gotten to the level where I could decide how things were done," he said. "I miss guiding the boat."

- I've even heard rumors that some people actually get tired of golf! I know that may sound absurd to some, but there you have it: I've heard rumors.

- In a letter to Dear Abby, "Searching for 'Me' in Texas" complained about "feeling worthless and guilty for being nonproductive." "Searching" went on to lament several failed attempts at finding a job substitute that fit.[1] You know the topic is of general interest when Abby not only prints her letter and responds, but also prints a variety of reader-response letters in the following days. Apparently, a lot of people have tried things to try to "revive my self-worth."

---

1   "Dear Abby" letter and response, March 4, 2012.

All of these folks wondered what retirement was all about, particularly when key components of what was important to them at work just disappeared. They felt they'd left something behind, or they'd missed out on something special that they didn't find when retirement came. Each one missed something important that had taken a few decades to achieve. Something that was meaningful. Something that was rewarding. Something was expected but not found when retirement came around.

Some retirees find an alien world waiting after the familiar landmarks are erased. What do you do in this new environment? How do you act? How do you make a difference? Where do you fit? How can you find that sense of belonging again?

Where do these feelings come from? Why is this happening? And, perhaps more importantly, what can you do about it? Answering these questions in a way that will make a positive difference for your retirement is what motivates my writing this book.

What do you do with all that time? You've spent a lifetime being task-oriented and dedicated. Poof. That need is gone. Are you going to wander around, groping for things to fill the emptiness?

A lot of people are affected by this loss. According to research, fully 60% of retirees between years two and 15 of retirement are either still "trying to figure out what to make of this time in their lives" (22%) or "admit being worried, bored, or sad" (40%).[2] You can avoid either scenario.

On the other hand, some people never go through this stage. They remain content and feel fulfilled without having

---

2   "The New Retirement Mindscape. A groundbreaking, comprehensive study of the retirement journey." Prepared by Ameriprise Financial in conjunction with Age Wave and Ken Dychtwald, Ph.D. and Harris Interactive, Inc. January 2006, http://www.ameriprise.com.

had a transition period. My friend Buddy said, "Retirement took me three seconds: I took a step out the door and crossed into retirement. I never looked back."

How did Buddy get through this without a sense of loss? Why do some come away clean while others seem mired for a while in a sticky, uncomfortable place? A great deal of the answer to this question has to do with preparation. Buddy had a plan!

He knew where he was going. Work had been a means to afford what Buddy was passionate about, what was meaningful to him. Take work out of the equation and he ended up with full-time meaning.

For you and me, preparation needs to shoot to the top of our retirement agenda. Where are we going? Where will we find our full-time meaning, our purpose?

So, just what do you do to "figure out what to make of retirement"? What do you do to avoid "being worried, bored, or sad"? What steps do you take to prepare?

Start here. This book is about preparation and possibilities:

- Where to start
- What to do
- Pitfalls to avoid

Reading this book is a positive step toward understanding what's to come, how to plan, and what to include in your plan.

You can come out of this post-retirement period with renewed energy and motivation. You can look forward to making a difference. You can feel the rewards again.

To help understand what is taking place, we'll talk, chapter by chapter, about several key issues:

- **Things They Don't Tell You at the Retirement Party**: Work gives you a great many things that may not be obvious to you until they're gone. Once they are gone, you may be caught by unexpected feelings of loss and then struggle to move forward. In the first chapter, we'll talk about the variety of benefits work provides that you may be surprised to find you miss, and we'll begin to steer you to new sources for reclaiming the good stuff.

- **What to:** If you want to keep the bad guys away, you have to head 'em off at the pass. You need to be proactive. But in our urgency to relieve the feelings of loss, it's easy to make mistakes. What are some choices you should avoid? Find out here. Then move forward to discover things to embrace and try instead.

- **How to:** You *can* avoid the loss; you can figure out what you want to make of retirement. The ideal here is to accept and love your autonomy: Halleluiah, you're the boss! This chapter gives positive steps to achieving success: how to start and how to go further.

- **Where to**: The evidence shows clear, doable ways to generate and maintain excitement, contentment, and joy in your life. Everyone is different. You can't expect to follow Sally's path and achieve Sally's result. Those are for Sally. You get to choose for *you*. And a wonderful world of options awaits you. Life is a gift of abundance; we'll point you in a multitude of directions to explore.

- **When to:** Retirement is not the one-size-fits-all environment pictured in the travel brochures—as pretty as they may be. We'll introduce you to retirement stages that make sense. And we'll talk about what preparation for retirement can look like.

Welcome to the adventure called retirement. Whether you've not yet turned in your notice or you're already an old hand at "being home for lunch," you are involved in a new, potentially exciting part of your life. My hope for you is that retirement becomes a fruitful, energizing, playful, and purpose-filled place.

If you find yourself reading this book, you already have a head start because you care enough to explore options. Let's do it!

Things They Don't Tell You at the Retirement Party

People approaching retirement frequently fill their conversation with all the things they *don't* like about work. Their friends quickly join the litany. To hear a lunch bunch talk about work sometimes is to wonder why they are there at all—it sounds so bad. In comparison, retiring is a veritable Shangri-la, freedom from all the inane, crazy, demeaning, demanding things nobody likes about work.

Don't get me wrong. I'm all for dumping inane, crazy, demeaning, demanding things. Put me in charge! Hire the dumpster. Who likes that stuff?

But is retirement going to be the opposite? Hmmm. Will retirement be a magic, "feel good" potion? Come on. Am I hearing a carnival barker in there somewhere trying to hawk the secrets of mysteries behind the veil? Well, step right up. Has he a deal for you!

Besides, haven't we seen this pattern of talk before?

Teenagers getting ready to leave the nest and go out on their own do the same thing: bad-mouth home. A few years later, home doesn't look so bad. They've gone through a natural process of preparing to separate from one thing to be able to move to something new in their lives.

Dredging up all the not-great things about work is also a well-worn way of preparing for separation and transition. You have to beat the drums before the band can play. It is a ritual.

However, work has been the *source* of many things in our lives that we often don't even realize, especially as we approach retirement. So we're taken by surprise by feelings of loss. It may not be the loss of work itself that we feel, rather it is the loss of the good things—not just a paycheck—that work supplies. We don't miss working, but we miss things we have taken for granted. Things we experience *through* work.

Some of us in retirement feel the loss keenly. Life isn't happening. An expectation isn't met. A familiar reward is missing. A valued skill is no longer useful, or no longer has meaning.

For others of us, the feeling is an undercurrent. We're not clear about what the losses are. We might not have known ahead of time that we liked "driving the ship" as my friend Terry expressed. He found that out only when the ship disappeared. We may not know what we expected to happen, but we unexpectedly feel sad.

For many retirees, work had meaning, which in itself is a new thing in society and history. You and I share a place in the first generation that went wholesale after careers that made a difference. We wanted to change the world and saw vocation as a tool in our arsenal that would impact society for the better.

How was this goal for work different? Before our time work rarely had "meaning." My dad never spoke of his work as a tool and dye maker. It was just work. Our grandparents would have been appalled at the notion of quitting a job because "it no longer had meaning." You weren't supposed to like work. You were just supposed to do it. "Take care of your family" trumped "take care of me."

You and I may several times have quit a job because it wasn't holding up to far-reaching goals we set for it. And, if we've not actually quit, we've been overheard saying, "I don't like the work I do." As if liking a job made a difference.

I know some folks who refuse to retire. I know several people who feel their jobs make a difference. I'm not surprised they don't want to give that up. Retirement destinations often appear unstructured and unrewarding compared with careers that are meaningful—and part of our lives right now.

So, for those leaving a fulfilling job, retirement can result in sadness, maybe anxiety, grief, and even depression. Retirement is literally a loss. If you happen to be one of those people who feel they make a difference, the sadness may be unexpected but understandable.

Retirement is a major transition. We have spent a great deal of our lives expecting to work, training for work, or working. And now work is gone? So, even if you're like my friend Buddy who "got into retirement in three seconds," you are likely to have to make some adjustment to no longer being in the work or career game. Work may not have been meaningful, you may actually like having it behind you, but at the same time, it certainly is gone!

At retirement, we leave a portion of ourselves behind. We have changed in a way that involves how we think of ourselves. We are no longer the person we were. A reorientation is needed, but it can't be achieved until we think about how to replace or to deal with what we left behind.

If you don't think this fundamental change won't hit you or it hasn't hit you yet, I'd like you to consider this situation: Here you are, a nicely retired person at a party. Things are going great. You meet somebody new, who asks,

"So, what do you do?"

You've heard that question countless times over the last decades. Heretofore, you've had an answer. But now you are retired. Who are you? What do you say?

The *expected* answer generally centers on a job or career. Do you have the expected answer? What will it feel like when you no longer are seen as a contributor, a breadwinner, a player in the game? You may feel sidelined, like a spectator at a game you used to be good at and were proud to play. Who are you, now? What's your **identity**?

Before you can move on, you need to examine where you've come from. What have you left behind? Let's talk about a few of the things.

Eight Surprising Things That Go Missing

Obviously, you've left a paycheck behind. You may not actually miss it too much on a financial level, but you may be surprised on a deeper level when it stops coming.

Earning power isn't called "power" for nothing. When you were younger, you had the capacity to earn a bit more—a promotion, a special project, a bonus, a second job. In retirement such options may not be possible. Knowing you no longer have that power can be frightening. You have less to lean on. It's not just the paycheck that is gone, it is the **power** that having a job brings.

So you may consider going back to work. But if you are like me, you just don't *want* to do that job anymore. I spent forty years designing and developing computer software. It was challenging, rewarding, interesting; but after forty years, I was tired of it! So, I decided to stop doing it.

And now that I've been retired for a while, my **marketable skills** are limited because I haven't kept up. In the software engineering business, a person can be out of date in six months to a year. I'm not likely to be able to get back in the field, even if I wanted to.

If you try to re-enter the job market, you really feel a loss when an employer passes over your gray-headed experience and wisdom in favor of a younger, more vigorous candidate— one who can be hired for half the cost! The young one is likely perceived as more technologically up to date, more innovative. Mix this attitude with our society's general devaluing of older people, and you begin to see why a potential employer may have marked your application "over-qualified."

When you can't get back in, you feel limited. If you are bypassed or replaced by a younger person, you may feel rejected. You may even feel lonely. You will certainly feel less able, which leads to feelings of meaninglessness.

I'm not saying this picture is the way things ought to be. You ought to be valued for your experience. Doors should swing wider for you because you know how these things should be done! Right? But, sadly, part of the competition you face when you try to re-enter is a bias toward youth. If not that, then a bias toward lower wages—new hires don't command your salary.

Additionally, you can feel powerless when you've lost your **network**. For thirty of my forty years, I was an independent consultant. That meant I kept my eyes and ears open for the next job around the corner. I had a set of friends I often paired with on jobs. I would ask for their help, and they'd ask for mine. While most of these people are still around, my technical credibility is shrinking. This reduction in marketability means that getting back in—even with my network—would be an uphill struggle. The door is closing.

To a consultant, the network is even more important because it is the closest thing to having a sense of belonging. When you jump from project to project and, usually, from employer to employer, your network is your lifeline to a **community**.

I was fortunate over the last eleven years of my career to be able to concentrate on the work of two clients. I came to know the people and what they were trying to achieve. I made friends. I was seen as a partner in the work. I belonged. And when I left, I lost both communities—the ties to my network and the ties to the people for whom I did the work.

You may feel a similar loss even if you work or worked for one employer. You too may miss that sense of **belonging** when the door closes behind you.

My wife, Crys, was one of those individuals who felt the reality of retirement when the paycheck stopped coming. This very symbolic loss struck her profoundly. She had worked hard to become a valued professional in a corporate world in an era when women in the workplace have routinely been undervalued. Clearly, earning a paycheck was, to her, more than just having money to pay bills.

The paycheck was a symbol for a whole constellation of job-related things. Work gave her life **meaning.** She was valued at work. She gave back at work. She was a contributor.

To be sure, the paycheck is significant on a survival level. It brings a sense of security. But in our culture it also represents a myriad of other things that center on who we are:

- The paycheck is a measure of **achievement.** You have spent years studying and honing a skill set. The paycheck symbolizes that accomplishment; it's a reward for getting better at something.
- The paycheck is a measure of **self-worth.** In this society, a bigger salary equates with being of greater value. Somebody out there thinks you are worth "the big bucks." Not hard to agree with the obvious, is it? With the big bucks I'm thinking I am worthy.
- The paycheck is a measure of **satisfaction**. You've put in effort and you get money out. Like a simple transaction, the more that comes out, the more you're satisfied that you've made a difference.

Of course, achievement, self-worth, and satisfaction are not necessarily tied to the paycheck—at least not totally tied to it. Your motivation may well be intrinsic; you may have internal measures that tell you that you did well, regardless of what is on the paycheck.

Losing the paycheck is largely just a pointer, a symbol of what is really gone: work, which has been a major *source* in your life of economic power, marketable skills, a network/community, belonging, achievement, self-worth, satisfaction, and meaning, in addition to identity.

Seven More Surprising Losses

Leaving work means leaving other things behind, as well.

For example, what happened to all those **friends** you had at work? Do they call or come by? Do you get together for lunch or after work at the favorite watering hole? Why did they disappear? What are you going to do about it? Besides, they're so out of tune with the losses you feel (because they still have what you've lost) that you have less in common to talk about. How can they be of **support** to you?

The reverse is true, as well. For a while after I retired, I was really interested in what was happening at work. But as the activities that had consumed my workdays fell away— the decisions, projects and priorities—I gradually lost touch. Now, my interest is more of a concern for the well-being of the company and people I value. I am increasingly more distant from the work that occupies their time.

The job may also have brought you **recognition** from your employers, your peers, or your customers. People may have acknowledged your abilities and successes through awards, bonuses, testimonies, and gratitude. But now all that is gone.

Some of us miss work because of the continuous learning the job both required and provided—information, insights, technology, skills, and even new ways of being. The ready incubator of **intellectual stimulation** is gone.

I also missed work because of the **challenge** it offered. I could twist the computer's tail and get things out of it that made a difference. I got energized being able to work through technical difficulties and solve the problems. I felt a sense of triumph. I took my little stone and challenged a giant! I did it every day. Most days I won.

Teresa Amabile and Steven Kramer, authors of *The Progress Principle*, say:

> *If we believe that our work is valuable and we are successful, then we feel good about this key part of our lives. If our work lacks value or if we feel we have failed at it, then our lives are greatly diminished.*[3]

---

3   *The Progress Principle*, by Teresa Amabile and Steven Kramer. Copyright © 2011 by Teresa M. Amabile and Steven J. Kramer. Published by Harvard Business Review Press.

I contend that, even if we *voluntarily* leave a job where we felt our work was valuable, we may still feel no less the failure.

A time of high unemployment and slowed economy can also contribute to feelings of self-doubt. These conditions add pressure on the emotions, particularly if you volunteered to retire, or, as we say, you "took retirement."

Retirement in a tight economic environment may feel less like a victory and more just plain foolhardy. You are giving up what a great many are desperately trying to gain. You're tossing in the towel, walking away, leaving the scene. And every one of these phrases carries personal connotations befitting a loser, ne'er-do-well, or vagrant. You might as well live on the street. You gave up your paycheck. You fool!

And unfortunately, not all the people who retire do so of their own volition. Margaret Vickers, in the School of Management at the University of Western Sydney, in Australia, makes an interesting observation about folks who've been downsized (laid off, fired, let go):

> *Being made redundant, especially without choice, regardless of associated financial gain, is likely to be a significant source of grief.* [4]

If you are one of the unfortunate "retired" folks who did not do so by choice, you may experience an emotional kick in the gut. The people Vickers interviewed reported being in shock when the announcement was made, of feeling betrayed by the situation, of undergoing trauma. The loss is not only the job but also the sense of **choice** and at least a bit of control of your own destiny.

Retired folks, no matter how they get there, also leave the **structure** behind. A job is not just about what you did, your

[4] "Journeys Into Grief: Exploring Redundancy for a New Understanding of Workplace Grief," by Margaret H. Vickers in the *Journal of Loss and Trauma*, Issue 14, 2009.

level of achievement, or even about being recognized for your work. A job also takes time. A worker usually spends eight hours a day at work and another 46–50 minutes per day commuting.[5] Add in time for lunch, hauling kids to daycare and back, and an odd errand or two in preparation for work and you have a large daily investment.

That time commitment is just the beginning. For many, work expands to fill even more space. Ten-hour days become normal, and these are known to stretch to twelve.

Needless to say, you don't have daily commute time in retirement. On the contrary, in retirement you can suddenly find your day filled with empty space, overflowing with time you never had before. How do you act? What will you do? What will get you up in the morning? Phew! Will you even bother to get up in the morning?

Retirement can present decisions you may never have had to face before. You *had* to go to school. You *had* to go to work. For much of that 60 years' worth of time you *had* to get out of bed! What do you do when the "have-to" goes away? Are you like my friend Marcia, who says, "I need something to do, or I'll stay in my jammies all day"?

So, what could we lose in retirement? Let's make a list:

- Identity
- Power
- Marketable Skills
- Network/Community
- Belonging
- Meaning
- Achievement

5   Gallup's 2007 annual Work and Education survey reported American workers had a 46-minute round-trip commute. The American Community Survey Reports for 2009 reports a round-trip time of 50.2 minutes.

- Self-worth
- Satisfaction
- Friends
- Support
- Recognition
- Intellectual Stimulation
- Challenge
- Choice
- Structure
- And sometimes income

And, what do we gain? A large hole in the day where work used to be.

Surprise!

Now, I'm not saying you will experience a sense of loss for all these. I sincerely hope that will not happen to anybody. But I do expect after a year or so in retirement, you will look back over that initial period and recognize a loss or two or three out of the lineup.

The answer to the loss you feel is not necessarily to go back to work or to stay on the job until you drop. The answer lies in finding new *sources* for the things you used to get from work. Things you don't think much about until they're gone.

Which puts the ball back in play. In the next chapter let's smack that ball back and forth on the issue of things to avoid and things to do as soon as retirement hits.

For You

Before you jump into the next chapter, you might want to take a look at our website and get a head start on that new elevator spiel—what you would say about yourself if you only had the time it takes to get from the 5th floor to the 1st on a fast elevator. You can no longer say things like

"I'm a third grade teacher."

"I do physical therapy at the VA."

What do you say about yourself now that you are retired? How will you express your identity—at least enough to keep a conversation going? You can find this item at

www.retireto.info/goforward/bookresources/

What to

Knowing you may experience a sense of loss is important. Let's chart a course to get through those feelings. Good things do lie ahead. The question that remains is how to get there. Before the end of this chapter, we'll focus on things you will want to do early in retirement, but we'll start here with the pitfalls, the shoals you need to steer around as you navigate these opening years of retirement.

What to Avoid

Busyness

Rushing to get through the feelings of loss is definitely a mistake. Rule 1: Avoid busyness. "I'm so busy now I don't know how I found time to go to work." How often have you heard that statement from a retired person?

I don't know about you, but I wonder what the statement really means. Jumping in to fill the void created when the job goes away is entirely too tempting. And, sadly, we can be disappointed with retirement some months or years later because we feel tied to activities that are no longer of interest, especially if we're still doing the things we started the month after work ended. Remember the 40% who ended up "worried, bored, or sad" 15 years after retirement?[6]

My friend John was one of those who talked about being busy. After a few months of my retirement, he'd say, "See, didn't I tell you you'd be so busy you wouldn't know how you ever went to work?" But on a different occasion he became a little more candid when he said, "I've filled the house with ships in a bottle. I don't know what to do."

Clare, a friend of ours, reported that her aunt assigned her newly retired, Ph.D.-in-chemistry husband the task of tracking the family coupons. That kept him off the streets to be sure, but what else did it do? It does sound like a case of concern jumping in to solve a problem: Husband won't have anything to do; coupons will solve the problem.

Personally, I'm willing to cut Clare's uncle some slack—I retired in part because I didn't want to program computers anymore! So, maybe he didn't want to do chemistry any longer or teach anymore or fight for another grant. But, with a Ph.D., I think it is safe to assume he's used to a higher level of mental challenge than tracking coupons usually requires. How is organizing coupons keeping him challenged? How long will it take before doing the coupons becomes unbearably boring?

---

6   "The New Retirement Mindscape: A groundbreaking, comprehensive study of the retirement journey." Prepared by Ameriprise Financial in conjunction with Age Wave and Ken Dychtwald, Ph.D. and Harris Interactive, Inc. January 2006, http://www.ameriprise.com

Unfortunately, even though they mean well, some friends or family members may be eager to help you with the jump, the leap into "busyness." Mostly out of concern for you (I hope), they are willing for you to

- Help with afterschool care for grandkids
- Be a volunteer at church (hospital, shelter, food pantry…)
- Shuttle folks to and from a variety of appointments
- Play cards
- Do projects around the house

Please. I'm not saying you shouldn't enjoy your retirement. In fact, in a few minutes I'm going to recommend that very thing! Go ahead and play cards. Play bingo. Enjoy crafts. Hang out with your friends.

I'm not saying you shouldn't volunteer for the church or take care of the grandkids or provide transportation or mow the lawn; I am just trying to warn you of the dangers of "busyness" as a measure of how you are dealing with loss.

These quick, easy ideas from friends to fill your time are one of those "beware of Greeks bearing gifts" things. Nature abhors a vacuum. Close friends or family members get worried about you if you seem to have checked out or you're not as busy as you were prior to retirement. They want to help.

If you are feeling loss, keeping busy is not the answer.

Because they also may need your help or know of someone who could use your help, you are the logical candidate. You're caught up in a perfect storm, a confluence of pressures that send you off in a direction not necessarily of your own choosing. You have time, and they think you have all the time in the world. They are eager to fill that time for you. And they say pleasantly, "Just the ticket now that you're retired. It will keep you busy so you won't be bored."

Oops. Evaluate each request: Is this a "busy" thing or a choice you'll be happy with? Perhaps a short-term agreement would suffice to help you decide.

Long-term contracts

But you know better, right? You want to evaluate the options. You want to try new things. Our second rule, then, particularly at the outset of retirement, is to sign no long-term contracts. Think of this time at the beginning as an incubation period. You're going to toss different things into the incubator and see what will hatch.

Everybody wants to "play more golf" when they retire, right? I've heard two different results.

On one hand, golf can be a letdown. I overheard this retirement golf story in the locker room: A man said he played golf almost every day for two years after he retired and got so sick of it he was sorely tempted to throw away the clubs. He said he might play now and again with his son, but he had to do something else.

On the other hand, my friend John got a job in the pro shop and got to play golf each and every day. All he could say was, "Please don't throw me into the briar patch!"

How do you know which scenario applies to you? You have to give yourself some trial time—maybe not two years, but enough time to evaluate the options.

My dreams of retirement included doing more with photography and, in particular, taking pictures of heavenly objects through a telescope. I think I overdosed on photography classes. I got into it enough to know I was not interested in investing great amounts of time at it. Photography remains a fun hobby, and I have a growing collection of nebula, star cluster, planet, and moon pictures to show for it. But it's not my "dream."

Maybe you should hold off settling on just one activity, thinking that it is "just the ticket" for the rest of your life. That big decision can wait until you have your "center" back and can honestly feel good about the choice.

Isolation

Avoid isolating yourself. If the majority of your social contacts were through work, retiring cuts those ties. You may suddenly find yourself alone, facing the loss of daily contact with coworkers and even customers. Isolation is a temptation. It is also a major threat to your health and well-being because isolation can easily lead to depression.

Don't hunker down in your cave and never come out!

On the surface, this advice seems like a contradiction. If I'm not supposed to keep "busy" with recommended tasks, won't the lack of activity look like I'm avoiding life? Won't making no commitments mean boredom?

Only you can evaluate these feelings. You have insider knowledge. The experiences are yours. What do they feel like?

Doing things that make you laugh, being with friends, and caring for family are important because they have intrinsic value. We'll talk more about intrinsic value later. But for now, keep in mind that these types of activities are important as touchstones. Loss or not, you probably still have friends and family and interests. Contact with people you enjoy will bring happy moments at a time when you may be struggling for clarity.

Invest in balance. Keep your friends close. At the same time…

Do take time for yourself—alone. Walk, listen, wait, evaluate. Ask yourself: Are the things I'm investing time in worth more of my time? What is it I'm really missing? What do I like to do? What have I not had the chance to do? How can I make a difference? Where will I find achievement, recognition, or satisfaction? Are these even important to me?

Introspection doesn't hurt. It just takes time. Don't avoid it just to keep busy. But don't let introspection consume your life, either. Balance in all things.

In the early days of retirement invest time in firming up your network of friends outside of work. A strong social network brings huge benefits. Having fun with friends is the ticket to fighting isolation.

I'm reminded of a recent TV ad for a type of automobile. The adult children are concerned because mom and dad don't have a bazillion Facebook friends, or they appear to be holed up and never go out. Meanwhile, mom and dad are out cavorting with friends, going biking and, by all appearances, having a blast. Shows what kids know!

If you've not seen the ad, not to worry. You could make your own ad, I bet. How long does it take you to coordinate a calendar date to have friends over? Between our activity schedules, writing and editing chores, and afterschool care for our grandson, calendars get crowded around our house. Our kids don't need to worry about us being holed up. They are more likely to have trouble finding us! We are definitely not isolated. I wish for you the same!

Overdoing one thing

A steady diet of anything becomes monotonous. This is true for food, drink, and maybe even golf. Work might even have gotten that way. Maybe, it is also true for anything we do in retirement if we overdo it. Avoid too much of one thing.

My son-in-law, Gary, reports that a family member of his spent the first ten years of his retirement watching motorcycle races on TV. Gary quipped, "I think he woke up one day and was surprised that he hadn't died yet and decided to get on with life after that." Good for Gary's relative!

My wife calls the goal "balance." Her career was fraught with stress: multiple deadlines to meet, six staff members to supervise, endless reports to prepare, new products to dream up, and too many projects to manage at one time. Too much to do. Too little time to do it.

When she retired, she took a project with her. One project. No staff. No budgets. Only one set of achievable deadlines.

She proudly maintains she "did the best work of her career" because it was the only work-related thing on her plate. In addition she painted our house. She did afterschool care for our grandson. She gardened. She rode her horse. Her life was balanced and consequently energized. Work was not all-consuming.

Hurrying

The last thing you want to avoid is rushing the result. It takes time to hatch an egg and even more to raise a fully developed fledgling. Give your choices some time. It took a while to get into your last gig, right? So, getting this one may take a while too. Also, you may discover more surprises that need some time to resolve.

When "the best work of her career" was done, my wife had a surprise. She was flabbergasted when she missed the paycheck. She is a thoughtful, intelligent woman and knew her self-worth was not really tied to a paycheck. Until the paycheck actually disappeared.

However, it was not the check itself she missed. It was the loss of all that the check represented. She had to take time to deal with the sense of loss. Did she expect these feelings? Of course not. Did she know what to do about them? Not really.

But she did some research. She found others who shared the experience and learned from them. The key ingredient for getting these feelings back to a balanced norm was time. Allowing yourself the time to work through the loss is critical.

One word seems to sum up what we find important in work: progress.

At the end of a workday, I want to be able to say, "Today I accomplished something." It doesn't have to be big. What I make progress in today does not in itself need to be important. But it is important to know that what I've done is on the right track for completing something I care about.

> To be meaningful, your work doesn't have to have profound importance to society.... What matters is whether you perceive your work as contributing value to something or someone who matters (even your team, yourself, or your family).[7]

We know how to do the "progress" thing. We just graduated from a career where we achieved it. We probably even miss it. So, we want, and maybe we even need, to dive in and achieve results! Quickly. We want to make retirement feel as good as making progress at work did.

Never mind you spent years getting ready to do the job. Never mind the additional decades it took getting good at it. Those preparation steps are forgotten in the frenzy to fill the void left by all the things that abruptly disappeared.

So, instead of preparing for retirement, you get busy. You hurry to find a replacement for work. You tackle one thing as though it were the single solution work used to be.

---

7   *The Progress Principle*, by Teresa Amabile and Steven Kramer. Copyright © 2011 by Teresa M. Amabile and Steven J. Kramer. Published by Harvard Business Review Press.

I know not making progress will ultimately result in feelings of loss. So I give in to filling the day instead of filling my life with something new. I may even fear the exploration in case the search turns up empty.

Don't give in. Feelings come unbidden. What you do about them, however, is a mark of character. You want not just to fill a day but to fill a day *well*.

Think of this time in retirement as an expectant time. It is a time between planting and harvest. You water and tend; in a while new growth will come.

What to Embrace

The time you have

Society doesn't help with this task much. It largely devalues people who've achieved these "advanced years." Here is how Art Linkletter defines "old":

> *If you're very lucky, you'll grow so old that morticians will follow you around with a measuring tape to save time. You'll need a fire marshal on hand for your birthday cakes. When someone mentions they spoke to you, people will gasp and exclaim "Is he or she still alive?" That's old.* [8]

The idea that older people had limits to their value started in the Great Depression. Here was born the notion that "old men should retire and make way for young men who needed to work to support their families."[9]

---

[8] *How to Make the Rest of Your Life the Best of Your Life*, by Mark Victor Hansen & Art Linkletter. Copyright © 2006 by Hansen & Hansen LLC and Art Linkletter. Published by Thomas Nelson.

[9] "William Osler and The Fixed Period," by Laura Davidow Hirshbein, M.D., Ph.D. Originally published in the *Archives of Internal Medicine*, Volume 161, September, 24, 2001.

At the beginning of the twentieth century, Doctor William Osler gained notoriety for his views on this subject when he made some remarks in his retirement speech from Johns Hopkins that led people to believe he thought men who had attained old age (67) should be chloroformed. Because he was a notable figure at the time, his remarks received wide attention. While he claimed he was not an advocate of this measure, his speech did largely advance the notion that young men are better and old men are useless.

In some cases, opinions go far beyond joking. More recently, Robert Butler reminded us:

> We find thoughtful pundits, economists, politicians, and policymakers who fear that societies will be unable to absorb the rising numbers of older people. They worry about the cost. They conjecture that added years of life will lead to intergenerational conflicts. They predict that the graying of society will lead to the stagnation of productivity.[10]

Butler concludes that these notions are stereotypes that do more harm than good.

With the advent of Social Security and increase in availability of company pension benefits, retirement gradually became the norm rather than the exception. But the legacy of opinion barely changed. If you don't work, you are of less value. I have an analogy for you:

> To be old these days is like being a rock on the side of the stream—because the rock lies to one side and is, for all intents and purposes, immobile, it holds little meaning for those in the swift-flowing stream going by. Hardly worth a glance if you are caught up in the rush called "the real world" and whisked off down-stream.

---

10 "It's Time for New Age Thinking," Robert N. Butler (Founder of the International Longevity Center), *AARP Bulletin*, Volume 29, #3, April 2008.

The truth is you may encounter even worse images of aging. Society often looks ahead toward retirement and sees a door. A final door. A door that ushers in the last days of life.

Abandon hope all ye who enter here.[11]

Printed on the entrance to hell, this inscription is a pitiless, dire warning against the painful consequence of a sin-filled life. The final pain is the absence of hope—for all eternity.

But whether you are a sinner or not, this description underpins our reluctance to talk about the retirement phase of life. Retirement for some means passing into our "end time." We dare not hope for more, as this is the end. We are reluctant to pass into that end time; so we refuse to talk about its encroachment.

The notion that retirement was the end held far into the twentieth century. My friend Tim worked as an executive in the steel industry. He reported that he regularly attended the funerals of retired executives between nine and 12 months after they received their gold watch.

This image of retirement largely ignores the possibility that retirement is more than an end. Fortunately, we don't need to treat retirement as *The End* these days. Our life expectancy has dramatically increased since Osler made his scandalous remarks.

You can claim full Social Security at a certain age. It was 66 for me, and it is being raised regularly over the next few years. Originally, this age was 65. This number was set in 1935 when Social Security was enacted. The life expectancy then was 58 for men and 62 for women.[12] What is this? Did anybody expect to pay out much of anything in the way of Social Security benefits?

---

11 *Divine Comedy*, Dante Alighieri, A.D. 1321.
12 "Life Expectancy for Social Security," Social Security History, www.ssa.gov.

Well, not if you check the numbers at birth. High infant and child mortality drove the rate down. The outlook improved the older you got. If you were a man and reached the age of 21, you were expected to be able to work long enough to contribute to Social Security and consequently to benefit for up to 13 years. Only a little more than half of all males in 1940 survived to the age of 65. Just fifty years later 72% were expected to.

Going from 50% to 72% means the number of people reaching retirement age is half again more than what it was in 1940. On top of that, if you reach age 65 in relatively good health, your reward is even longer life.[13] Compared to 60 years ago, more older adults can expect to live longer. We've made progress in longevity.

> **Don't stop now!**
>
> Today, you have a life expectancy of 19-plus years if you reach the age of 65. This is more than a five-year increase over the life-expectancy age in statistics collected in 1950; the average then was just under 14 years.

The gravediggers need to catch up with the times! Retirement has fewer limits than those naysayers would allow. Retirement should not be limited to last rites. Today, retirement is not an end; it is a beginning. As my friend Brian told me over the phone the other day, "We got twenty years of life that is unscripted."

My hope is that you will embrace the time you actually have. You probably don't have half a century, but the amount of time you have is not trivial. On the other hand, you don't want to waste what you do have by making repeated wrong turns. We need a plan to get it right. That's the ticket. And it starts with…

---

13 19.2 is average for all races, male and female in 2009. A chart prepared by the Centers for Disease Control and Prevention in 2011. See the chart at www.cdc.gov.

Fun

Every kid in the universe can probably tell you that the opposite of work is...

Wait for it...

PLAY!

Gee, that sounds great! When I quit work, I can play! What a great notion. It is heartwarming and absolutely critical to retirement. As retirees, you and I need to embrace our sense of play again. Dr. Stuart Brown, the author of a book about play, says:

> *We do not stop playing because we are old; we grow old because we stop playing.*
>
> *—Anonymous*

> [Play] energizes us and enlivens us. It eases our burdens. It renews our natural sense of optimism and opens us up to new possibilities.[14]

If retirement isn't a place for renewal, optimism, or new possibilities, I don't know any better one. Play is a survival mechanism for humans, as it is in much of the animal kingdom.

It's not really true, you know: That bit about the opposite of work being play. Why? Because Dr. Brown insists that the opposite of play is not work, but depression. Isn't that interesting?

At this stage of life, in the major transition called retirement, it is not uncommon for people to feel a large sense of letdown. More than a little worry and less than full-blown depression, this period may be a time when we

- **Feel confused:** Old ways of being no longer fulfill and may even be unavailable. We don't know what will come next.

14 *Play: How It Shapes the Brain, Opens the Imagination, and Invigorates the Soul*, by Stuart Brown. Copyright © 2009 by Stuart Brown. Published by Penguin Group.

- **Question our adequacy:** Why is retirement such a hard thing? Other people retire without a blink. Something's wrong with me.
- **Question our coping skills:** I must be getting lazy. I'm fearful—what's with that?
- **Hide our feelings:** I can't share the fact that I feel inadequate. I'm a full-grown adult. I should be able to deal with this matter on my own. Besides, what could someone else do to help these feelings? They are not experiencing the feelings themselves.
- **Retreat from social contact:** I don't feel like going out. The stuff they do just doesn't interest me any longer. My friend means well, but she can't help me.

Psychologists have an image and name to describe this period: the fertile void. Psychotherapist Nancy Shepherd says, "The fertile void is essentially a time of waiting, not acting."[15] She goes on to say, "Ultimately, the fertile void is an opportunity to reconnect with the essence of who we are and how we want to be in the world."

The fertile void is a time of engagement. You may not know what the next step will be, but waiting is a step of courage and not one of retreat. That doesn't make waiting any easier:

> For a culture on the go all the time, such a concept may seem not only impractical, but also unachievable. Today, we measure our worth by what we do and how busy we are. That's why it's so difficult to disengage ourselves from all manner of electronic gadgetry when we go on vacation.[16]

Shepherd says this waiting can be unnerving, and you may feel fearful. The road is not clear. Control seems elusive at

---

15 "Feeling Lost and Confused? Time to Explore the Fertile Void," by Nancy Shepherd, M.Ed., *Vitality Magazine*, February 23, 2012.

16 "Feeling Lost and Confused? Time to Explore the Fertile Void," by Nancy Shepherd, M.Ed., *Vitality Magazine*, February 23, 2012.

best. Your common touchstones are tumbling, and you feel unstable on what used to be solid ground.

Your feelings may be worse than feelings of inadequacy or confusion.

> *Moving [or retiring] to a new place may be your own idea, but that doesn't mean you won't get overwhelmed and depressed wondering if you've made a big mistake. You have to expect that all change is going to have lots of struggle, not just rewards.*[17]

If your feelings become physical problems—inability to sleep or sleeping too much, unexplained headaches or pain, sudden and surprising outbursts or crying—you need to evaluate carefully. Do these unwanted symptoms persist? How long have they lasted? Are they anchored in recent events? Are you experiencing other traumas in your life?

I have aches and pains. Combined with increased brain stimulation *(What is the next chapter of this book going to look like?)*, I can easily lose sleep. I'll either have a hard time going to sleep or wake in the middle of the night and not be able to get back to sleep. My head is squirreling with ideas and notes and notions; I often just give in, get up, and write them down while I can still remember them.

When I look at my lack of sleep, I take circumstances into account. If you have unexpected and unwanted feelings, or symptoms like sleeplessness, do the same. Assess what else is going on for you. Illness of a friend? Death of a loved-one? Tough time for somebody close? Do you have a new illness? Have you started a new exercise regimen? After all, your body has many parts that seem only to make themselves known when you use them.

---

17 "The Link Between Depression and Expectations," by Rhoda Mills Sommer, L.C.S.W., January 15, 2012, http://relationshiprealities.wordpress.com.

But if the lack of sleep, headaches, or unexpected emotions escalate or persist, you should seek help. Find a qualified individual who can help you sort out your feelings and symptoms. Appendix A can provide initial assistance with identifying signs of depression and knowing what to ask someone who can guide you.

> **Danger**
> *If you feel like hurting yourself or someone else, call 911 and get help right away.*

People cope differently with the changes retirement brings. As I mentioned earlier, managing the transition took my friend Buddy three seconds—he didn't feel a loss at all. But my wife entered the fertile void two years after her retirement. Resolution may take longer for you than for someone else, and the severity of your feelings about the changes and loss may be very different from the feelings others experience.

The transition is real. You move from a job or career to retirement and discover retirement is "in a different building." You may feel a need to find a solution. You may hope to make a big change. You'll naturally be curious about what a "second adulthood" might resemble. You are moving from one place to another—expect some travel time.

Think of this time as one of lying fallow. The field has been plowed, but not yet planted. It seems empty. No crop is growing, but something equally important is going on.

This time of lying fallow—of waiting—is still productive. In the fertile void, the weeds are destroyed and the land regains its fertility. New life can emerge.

How long is this struggle going to take? Unfortunately, there is no rule of thumb. A fallow field is usually left for a "season," which can be different for everyone.

On the bright side, you may not experience anger bordering on rage, severe depression, or the acute denial that plagues others. I hope you don't. But, the fertile void seems to start with the recognition that a change is needed and ends with an embrace of the future. The timeline between the two varies.

Suzanne Braun Levine popularized the notion of the fertile void in her book, *Fifty Is the New Fifty*.[18] In one of her many online videos, she talks about the one- to two-year time frame for finding yourself again with your feet on the ground.

It took our good friend Lanette a year to come out and smell the roses again. She just needed time to decompress. She wasn't depressed, but neither did she feel like meeting the neighbors or doing anything in particular.

On the other hand Lynda reports:

> *After nine months of not doing anything career-oriented, focusing on fixing up my house, doing little decorating projects I'd put off for years, cleaning out closets, taking some short trips abroad, having lunch with my girlfriends for the first time in many years, doing some cooking, enjoying my kids, I suddenly understood what I wanted to do. I gave birth to myself—again.*[19]

Sadly, we are limited to anecdotal information. Which can be good if you resolve your situation before the "deadline" claimed by the anecdotes you've heard. Or, you can feel worse if you've trundled past the hoped-for end points with no light visible at the end of the tunnel.

So, in the meantime take your medicine: Play! It is the opposite of depression.

---

18 *Fifty Is the New Fifty: Ten Life Lessons for Women in Second Adulthood,* by Suzanne Braun Levine. Copyright © 2009 by Suzanne Braun Levine. Published by Penguin Group.

19 "Fifty Is the New Fifty—Lynda's Time in Limbo," by Suzanne Braun Levine, July 8, 2009, www.suzannebraunlevine.com.

Newfound freedom

In his TED talk in 2009, author and speaker Daniel Pink advocated for autonomy as a key element in motivation. People who are self-directed are much more able to solve complex problems.

Now, I'm not necessarily advocating you go out and solve the world's most complex problems as something to do in retirement. Although, if you have the wherewithal to do so, have at it! The world needs more solutions.

I remind myself that I am already faced with a complex problem: retirement itself. How do you reorder a day that used to be structured by someone else? What do you do now that you are not working toward goals someone else has set? How will you do anything without someone watching and maybe criticizing your every step?

But at the same time, in retirement you don't have to look over your shoulder. How wonderful is that? And how often have you longed for just that very thing: Not having a boss to organize your every minute or micro-manage your life down to a nib?

Well. Good news. You are retired. You have the say so. You get to structure your day.

Embrace the freedom.

The trick is, of course, that you may not have had this level of freedom since you were a kid. As a kid you could wander off on your bike and come home at dinnertime. In the meanwhile go fishing, hiking, explore a creek, or play softball. You could go with friends or wander alone. Library? Build a fort in the woods? Play Hide and Seek in the barn? Hopscotch? Kick the Can? Chase the dog? Find the new kittens?

Remember that time? Well, it may take some time to reclaim a sense of play. It will most certainly take time to let playfulness be in control as it was in that earlier point in our lives. I had to rid myself of the worry about what was on the other end of the holiday. How do you get to a point of *not* having to plan to be back somewhere, to attend something, to tend to something? Let play be it! Be free again.

My wife, Crys, and I have led quite a few workshops on retirement issues. I like the Lunch and Learn program we call Retirement 101. This thirty-minute to an hour program starts with *Musical Chairs,*[20] a short video that uses the game as a metaphor for retirement. Stop when the music stops— try golf. Stop when the music stops—try Bridge. And so on. Knitting. Vacation. The movie showed a big circle of chairs with lots of stereotypical images of retirement offerings.

The hero of the movie finds this projection of retirement oppressive. As would I! He runs from it! As would I! He doesn't know what he's running to.

Therein lies the rub. What will he run to?

What to Try

As an investigation policy, I welcome the concept: Try this; try that. What feels good? So, I suggest two key starting points.

Making space

I worked until 10 p.m. the last day at the office. I tried to finish that last task and make it "just so." I didn't want to leave a poor product behind as a remembrance.

The next morning at dawn, my wife and I were off to the airport for a trip to Boston. It was a much-anticipated trip. We made lists of things to do. We had special sleeping arrangements: We stayed on a boat in the Boston harbor, a floating bed-and-breakfast. What fun that trip was! We did

---

20 *Musical Chairs*, Developed by Dr. and Mrs. Richard Bergstrom of Church-Health and LifeTime Ministries. www.Re-Ignite.net.

the tourist thing and followed the red brick walk around the city, had dinner in Chinatown and Little Italy. We saw the Fine Arts Museum and Paul Revere's house.

Hey. We unwound Ed, who, as it turned out, needed unwinding very much.

I know to recommend travel to retirees is a cliché. But I've discovered a compelling reason for it. You have to give in to play to find a freer you. You have to make space for a new you to emerge.

Making space for the new meant something different for our friends Carole and Foye. They made space by moving to a new location. Part of that transition was clearing out the old stuff, sorting through the past, in order to make room for the future.

Our friend Susan, a retired pastor, has a new ministry/ business helping people "clear the way home." She sees people's lives change for the better when they can take charge of the accumulated things of the past and declutter. By making physical space in their homes, they also open emotional space to be able to go forward in their life.[21]

Exploring options

In high school, I took up photography. I had vowed I would delve into my hobby again when I retired. And, as I mentioned earlier, I did exactly that.

Did this effort meet expectations? Not so much. I did accomplish part of what I wanted; I have better equipment and I take better pictures. But I ended up with the same level of interest as before. Was I glad I did it? Absolutely. It was fun. I overdosed on photography classes for about a semester and had a ball.

---

21 Clearingthewayhome.com.

My friend Susan had just the opposite experience. She dived into photography, and we haven't seen her since. She barely comes up for air. In photography, she found a new passion.

So, if you are working through the fertile void and trying to get a handle on life's next direction, I have a single-word solution for you: play. Try an old hobby. Visit an old acquaintance. Delve into this and that. Give yourself some time off and permission to fiddle with the knobs. It won't hurt to get your hands dirty.

The time for deep investment can wait until you see a clearer path. Maybe you'll continue down the path started by one of these trials. Maybe not. But, if you pick fun things to do, your time will not have been wasted.

Here are some playful ideas that have worth even if no new lifetime goals emerge:

Road Scholar: My wife and I are making plans to take our nine-year-old grandson on a five-day excursion. The Road Scholar program offers courses all over the world on a huge variety of topics. The bulk of the activities involve both grandparents and grandkids. We look forward to horseback riding,[22] swimming in the Gulf of Mexico, seeing an alligator farm, going to the zoo, and seining in Weeks Bay with our grandson. We'll have at least one night when the kids will go off together to plan their skits while the grandparents hear a lecture about the history of the area.

Any of these courses may influence a new passion. But even if they don't, I will have had an interesting adventure. Planting memories is a good thing.

---

22 Well, some of us do. My wife is the rider in the family, and our grandson will often gladly do what his grandmother asks. That leaves me. Have you heard the "Epic Tale of My Last Ride"? The short form goes something like this: It didn't go well.

Vacations: The Road Scholar organization has a wide variety of programs but can't cover the waterfront. Have you always wanted to go horseback riding but never could? Try a dude ranch. Ever hiked the Appalachian Trail? Why not participate in an archeological dig? A former acquaintance took off for China to teach English as a second language for a year. Twelve months might be a little longer investment than you want, but it did give her lots of time and an income to explore a new culture.

Courses: Schools and universities in many areas offer night classes or lectures on a variety of topics. I've taken writing classes, computer classes, how to do an elevator spiel, writing more effective nonfiction (I hope it shows), an iPhone class, and more. Crys took classes in gardening, cooking, and writing. You can try your hand at whatever tickles your fancy. Give your inner potter's wheel a whirl. Touch up that canvas with a little paint. Groom your dog. Cook Cajun, French, or Chinese or just cook better.

You could end up investing a lot of time with any of these later. For now, you can find out what works and feels good. Play is its own reward.

Volunteer or part-time work: Long ago, my daughter played solitaire, days and days and hours and hours of solitaire. She had graduated from college, spent another year on a Fulbright fellowship, and had bounced back to live with us. She was a boomerang kid before boomerang kids were invented. You know the problem: What to do with life?

Solitaire. The obvious choice.

At the same time she had a part-time job in an upscale retail store and a volunteer position at a daycare for disadvantaged children. She seesawed back and forth. By day she met society's hidden people—folks with few resources, limited prospects, and seemingly bottomless need. By night she assisted customers who were quite willing to part with a portion of their seemingly limitless discretionary income.

She passed her time in the fertile void playing solitaire, working part-time, and volunteering. She ended up going to graduate school. Did she ever work retail again? No. Does she do hands-on client-related work? No. She made a different choice, but the paid and non-paid work experiences set her new direction. While she could do the work, neither floated her boat.

Speaking of "floating the boat," isn't that what we're about here? Looking for what will get you up in the morning, keep your interest, hold your attention?

Caution: Don't shoot yourself in the foot

Don't talk yourself out of trying things. Trying things pushes the limits on our fear responses:

- I don't know how
- I can't learn how
- I can't compete
- I don't want to be like the Joneses

When you focus on these and not on what you want to accomplish, you rob yourself of energy and motivation, putting up a barrier between you and trying. Isn't that what fear does to us—makes us run, hide, and put something between us and the threat?

I grant that dragons are out there. Some may even be after me. But I learned long ago to distinguish between real threats and the imaginary ones I make up myself. I'm OK with a threat when I can keep it under the bed.

At the same time an odd thing about fear is that you can't fear fear, either. Some self-doubt is crucial for success. I cannot improve if I don't catch on to the fact that I'm behind the curve. According to Daniel Pink, some self-doubt is not all bad. He reports on a study that introduced self-questioning before delving into a task.[23] The groups that asked, "Can I?" achieved better results than the ones saying, "I Can." Counterintuitive? Maybe so. The trick is to walk the fine line and not run pell-mell away from trying.

Being critical of yourself and bringing your critical thinking skills to bear on ideas can be healthy. But what you should avoid is what author and blogger Dragos Roua calls "the black power of no."[24] Negativity drains your energy and robs you of your willingness to move forward. What you're trying to embrace is the chance to improve at what you do.

Who knows? At the end of what we're exploring here, or at the very least, after you've pursued all the options this book recommends, you may actually find yourself very busy. Good. It won't be the same kind of busy we started this chapter talking about. It will mean you're invested in things that mean the most to you.

Let's talk more about where to start and how to find the right match of meaningful activity for you.

---

23 "Motivating Goal-Directed Behavior Through Introspective Self-Talk," by Ibrahim Senay, Dolores Albarracin, Kenji Noguchi. Copyright © 2010 by the authors. Published in *Psychological Science*, April 2010. Daniel Pink reported this in his *Flip Manifesto* published via PDF: http://danpink.s3.amazonaws.com/FLIP-Manifesto.pdf.
24 "Positive Motivation Versus Negative Motivation," by Dragos Roua, posted on www.dragosroua.com, July 2009.

For You

Let's explore some options about what your day will look like in retirement. I took the easy road when I retired—I asked people what they did all day. Some answers really surprised me! Some people didn't do much. Well, that wasn't very appealing.

What might your friends be doing in their retirement? I've listed some questions you can use to interview your friends—formally or informally. Explore what your day might look like by finding out what others do.

www.retireto.info/goforward/bookresources/

How to

In establishing a new aim in life, the first task is to assess the current reality. You need to understand your starting place. Think of this effort as placing your feet in the starting blocks: You don't want to begin a race without a good stance.

The assessment will ultimately help you uncover what motivates you and find the sometimes-hidden values that rest at the core of who you are. In this task you will examine points in two categories:

1. Get these out of the way
   Finances
   Unfinished business
2. Focus on these
   Identity
   Keystone habits
   A new boss
   Targets and goals

Get These Out of the Way

Finances

The motive in reviewing finances at this point is simple: In order to be at peace with your retirement, you need to know whether you're "making it" moneywise. With a paycheck out of the picture, understanding your new norm is vital to your comfort. So is knowing when some action may be needed.[25]

As a starter, in which of these three categories would you place yourself?

- I don't have to worry.
- I could get in trouble, so I have to be careful.
- I'm going to need another source of income.

You see what I mean about "understanding the starting place." If a part- or full-time job is necessary, your options for retirement activities are limited; some of your active day will have to be spent at work. If you are living within your means but have to keep tabs, part of your retirement will be spent record-keeping.

The task of assessing your financial well-being may be unfamiliar. Basically, it has to do with keeping track of how much you spend and for what. If you are unfamiliar with how to do that, please take a look at Appendix B for a primer.

The financial challenge of retirement is to keep "making it." While it's probably a no-brainer to you, it was worth an honorable mention to Verne Wheelwright, a notable futurist:

---

25 How you treat finances can be revealing. Much of the "scripts" you use to pattern your behaviors in spending are partly inherited and partly learned at a very early age. Do you avoid risks or take too many? Underspend or overspend? A good resource to help you understand your behavior is *Wired for Wealth*, by Brad Klontz, Psy.D., Ted Klontz, Ph.D, and Rick Kahler, CFP. Copyright © 2008 by Brad Klontz, Ted Klontz, and Rick Kahler. Published by Health Communications.

"One effective strategy is to learn, at any age, to live below your means."[26]

So, as you assess the big picture of your finances, be sure to understand the little picture as well: Where is your money going? Don't let the answer to that question be a surprise. You can often take steps to curb some expenses, but only if you know which ones are making an impact. To live below your means requires information.

Unfinished business

It is unfortunate, but in the past several years of economic turmoil, some companies have decided their "solution" is downsizing employees with the most experience. Generally higher paid, these individuals find themselves at the peak of their career for the skill they have, but at the bottom of the heap in terms of reemployment. Being without work at age 50+ is tough indeed.

Being downsized at that age is harder than losing your job at a younger age. You may find yourself thinking about retiring rather than trying to land a new job or start a new career. Although you may have already begun to ask the transition questions about retirement, generally, you are not mentally prepared to answer them. After all, you likely had no warning your time had come.

Reemployment may also be near to impossible if the profession you had has undergone changes. I know former typesetters whose industry evaporated when computer technology took over. My graphic artist friends have lost work (and complain of the lack of standards) in the current do-it-yourself, it's-good-enough workplace culture. And don't ask me how many grammatical errors I see daily on

---

26 "Strategies for Living a Very Long Life," by Verne Wheelwright. *The Futurist,* November–December 2010.

billboards, ads, and articles including newspapers, once famed for editorial precision. I know videographers without work. And we all know of the hordes of blue-collar workers with no assembly lines available.

If an upside to this situation exists, it begins with introspection. The usual approach is to retool. Go back and get a certification or degree and, thus armed, find a new job. This method may work for some people, even those who "got volunteered" to retire. Retooling can cost money and even years with no guarantees of results. With introspection, however, some folks have begun reinventing themselves instead of investing in the usual pattern of retooling.

Author Gail Sheehy puts such firings in a different perspective:

> ...it turns out to be just what they need to shift from a laser focus on outer success to a discovery of the foreign realm of their inner lives.[27]

She reports specifically about the transition made by Lee Kravitz, editor-in-chief of *Parade Magazine* until he was fired in 2008. In his words: "My identity was my work. My role in the world was my work. I lost sight of who I really was."

Kravitz has gone on to write a book called *Unfinished Business,* which profiles ten journeys he took to get back in touch with who he was and who he is. He discovers "that the things we let slip are exactly those that have the power to transform, enrich, enlarge, and complete us."[28]

The book contains a number of other people's stories as well as his own.

27 "At 54, He Lost Job But Gained Perspective, Compassion," Gail Sheehy, *USA Today*, 2/7/2011, usatoday.com

28 *Unfinished Business: One Man's Extraordinary Year of Trying to Do the Right Things,* by Lee Kravitz. Copyright © 2010 by Lee Kravitz. Published by Bloomsbury. myunfinishedbusiness.com.

As retirees, we owe a debt to the Lee Kravitzes of the world for having faced the problem—even though they had to do so without any of the preparation we can draw on. It doesn't matter whether they voluntarily retired or not. Let's give them some due and consider their bed-rock question: Who am I?

Recently, my wife and I intentionally explored my past and hers. We visited some of my graduate school buddies and some of her college friends. We talked about their choices in retirement, as well as ours. These visits brought back memories, inspired us, and also challenged and fed our future plans.

Fortunately, we've not discovered any regrets in these wanderings, which Kravitz did. Apparently he

- Was a workaholic
- Ignored his wife
- Had no relationship with his children
- Made commitments he didn't keep
- Ignored his few relatives

Do you find yourself in this list? How might you meet those regrets? Kravitz planned and executed several trips to see what he could do about the things he figured were mistakes. He found the trips to be healing for him and for those with whom he met.

During the early phase of your retirement, it wouldn't hurt to plan your own odyssey. Maybe it is time to go to that high school reunion. Do you have regrets, owe debts, need forgiveness, or want to renew relationships? Planning to resolve these early in retirement is a good way to kick off the season.

A while back (25 years ago, actually), my mother saved my 25th high school reunion invitation for me. She wanted to be sure I attended. It seems she had just been to her 50th high school reunion and didn't remember anybody. She didn't want me to have the same problem. So, I made a promise to her: "I won't go to my 25th reunion, *and* I won't go to my 50th either!"

Saying I'd skip both was cute, so I thought when I said it, but I'm rethinking that commitment. To be sure, I don't recognize any pictures of current classmates shared on Facebook. But my curiosity is piqued. I'd like to find out what the new season of retirement has in store for my early friends.

You don't want to wait and perhaps shouldn't have waited earlier when your concern first became evident. But here you are. Now you can do something.

First, you need to get in touch with yourself. Do you have regrets or lingering concerns from the past? Executive coach Teresa Pool suggests several strategies, but to start, you can look for clues. Do you

- Dwell on a past conversation or incident?
- Have increased negative feelings or actions towards someone who has no clue as to why?
- Feel an emotional heaviness or avoidance around an unfinished project?
- Repeatedly play out a difficult conversation in your head?
- Avoid a specific person or situation?[29]

Now comes the challenge: Move the energy you used for avoidance to focus on and resolve the issue. The chief problem is getting around the fears of not doing it right, rejection, or consequences.

Psychotherapist Rhoda Sommer suggests that these leftovers haunt us. We can't move forward for being stuck

---

29 "Unfinished Business—The Power of the Un-done," Teresa Pool, transitionsforbusiness.com.

in the past. To take care of any "unfinished business," she advises talking to folks before they die and it is too late. She encourages telling the truth about feelings of anger or resentment and saying a final goodbye to someone so new relationships can bloom. She suggests writing a letter as a first step on the road to resolution.[30]

You may not actually have to send the letter to get results.

The good news in all this hard work is the benefits. We recover future time that would have been lost to regret or avoidance—because we won't be regretting any longer. But, if forgiveness is involved in your unfinished business, letting go of grudges and resolving disputes can even improve your health, lowering your blood pressure and heart rate. It may reduce chronic pain and ease symptoms from anxiety, depression, or stress."[31]

Focus on These

Identity

You are unique.

You can begin your exploration of options in retirement without knowing your motives, of course. It matters little to the universe if you are enjoying what you're doing. But if you want a rewarding retirement, you may want to look at who you are and what gets you up in the morning.

If you are in fact content being invested in a retirement activity because you like the

> *Keep in mind that the person to write for is yourself. Tell the story that you most desperately want to read.*
>
> — Susan Isaacs

---

30 "The Power of Unfinished Business," by Rhoda Mills Sommer, Relationship Realities, http://relationshiprealities.wordpress.com June 25, 2011.

31 "Forgiving Others Can Benefit Your Health," by Statepoint Media. Published in *Mature Lifestyles*, September, 2008.

challenge or affirmation, the reward or the work itself, you may very well be good to go. An ancient maxim about work sheds some light:

> *If you like what you do, you'll never work a day in your life.* —*Confucius*

So, if you were fortunate to have been able to do what you like, you may have a pattern you are perfectly comfortable with. My former doctor loved being a doctor. He worked into his 80s. He literally never retired. At age 85, he admitted to me he could no longer keep up and hadn't a clue of what he'd do in retirement. With tears in his eyes he said, "I've never done anything else in my life."

He was much like my wife. She loves editing. She'll probably do it until she can't read any more.

Neither Buddy nor I wanted to continue our careers, however.

So, where are you on that spectrum?

Finding out where you want to invest your time can be fun. My wife, for example, continues to be asked to do various editing projects throughout the year. She's good at those skills. She could simply continue doing work she has enjoyed professionally for more than 30 years.

However, retirement gave her the opportunity to examine where she wanted to go and what she wanted to do, based on who she is. One tool she used in her search was the "Drivers" survey.[32] The results showed her that mentoring was one of her top-five drivers, a value that gives her energy and meaning.

Consequently, Crys has developed a way to combine her editorial skill with her love of mentoring. She has set up a system for helping high school students write better.

---

32 *Don't Retire, Rewire,* by Jeri Sedlar and Rick Miners. Copyright © 2007 by Jeri Sedlar and Rick Miners. Published by Penguin Group.

So, what might you find out in your search? Whatever it is, it will

- **Likely show a relatively unique set of motivators**: We are all created equal. But only you are you. In absolute terms you and only about 2,200 other people in all of the United States are likely to share the same set of values.[33]

- **Highlight things you didn't realize were important to you**: Crys discovered just how high mentoring was on her list.

- **Weed out things you had previously thought important**: I always thought problem solving would rank near the top for me. I am good at it in the software arena. I enjoyed problem solving during software development. My surprise was that it didn't rank as high as I thought.

Good tools, such as the Drivers survey can help you uncover more about yourself so you can make decisions for how you reinvest. When your activity—your new "work"—flows from values you hold dear, then you'll be living the wisdom of Confucius.

Keystone habits

Don't laugh please; but I want to announce *the* key for your retirement day:

Make your bed.

Yep. That's the recommendation I'm reading in articles about happiness. Surprising? Well, it certainly was to me. Who knew?

Apparently author Karen Miller did. She wrote, "The state of your bed is the state of your head." This little act creates a welcome-

---

33 The chance of getting the same top 5 values out of a set of 30 is 1 in 142,506. According to the census bureau, we started 2012 with 312.8 million people in the United States. In a metropolitan area of a million and a half people, the size of Nashville, I might find 10 people who share the same 5 choices.

home statement at the other end of the day. An enthusiast for the concept of mindfulness, Karen insists the simple act of making your bed slows down what threatens to become another frenetic day.[34]

Your retirement day need not repeat the feverish and often frenzied schedule that often accompanies normal workdays. Retirement is not an exercise in "shove it all in and get it all done." It can be a time of life with more balance. My wife values this as she prefers a little of this and a little of that and not too much of any one thing. Gardening, riding the horse, playing with the grandson, volunteering, exercising, working some—mix a little of each and none in a big hurry. Stir carefully.

Mindfulness is about paying attention. Particularly: Slow down and pay attention.

In general, in your early retired years, you want to set up a new pattern for your day. You had to have a structure to get to work on time, attend to your family and household obligations, and also get in enough rest. The only difference may be that you don't want to emphasize one thing as much in retirement as you did with work.

Set up a daily schedule as you did before. Mix in a little of this and a little of that. Figure out what your day will be like. You don't have to end up with the same plan you start with. Experiment. We're back to play.

It is the regularity you want to achieve. But the new routine needs to include good habits and not just habits by default. Our friend Marcia insists she would lounge around in her pajamas and do nothing if given the chance. She wants

---

34 "10 Tips for the Mindful Home," by Karen Maezen Miller, January 2013, huffingtonpost.com. Karen is the author of *Hand Wash Cold: Care Instructions for an Ordinary Life* and *Momma Zen: Walking the Crooked Path of Motherhood.*

to have something to look forward to; otherwise, she fears becoming a couch potato. She needs structure.

That's what I mean by default. Too much TV. Overkill on the computer. The computer and television can be great in small doses, but if drawn out, the two can be deadening distractions and meaningless entertainment. Sadly, the TV remote and computer mouse can become what passes for retirement choices for some folks. I would not wish that for me. Or for you.

But here are some ideas to get you going in good directions:

Start of the day: Make a good breakfast part of your start every single day. And, if you want to follow the advice given above, make your bed.

Then, start the day with something to do. Make it a planned and often regular thing. My wife and I exercise six days a week. Most of the time, the exercise starts the day. Other folks I know start certain days with some volunteer activity. The start of the day is the place to put that part-time (or full-time) job.

If you have to work, I do encourage you to be selfish. You may not have been able to wedge exercise into your workday prior to retirement. Make every possible effort to do so now, during retirement. Even if you have to work to make ends meet, this time around invest part of your day in you.

Middle of the day: Be sure to have lunch.

You want to get up and out of the house every day. If Crys and I need to do grocery shopping, we generally do it after lunch. Doing errands is another example of getting up and out. You don't want your home or apartment to turn into a cave. Hibernation is for bears.

Besides, my friend Terry insists driving around town when all the employees are safely tucked away in their workplaces is refreshing—so much less traffic. Not to mention that the clerks you find may actually know what they're talking about because they have the seniority to make the junior help work at night and on weekends. Yeah! A butcher who can actually give you helpful advice.

So, start thinking of the middle of the day as a secret retiree resource. It is the place you can put all those errands you used to dread doing in the evening or on the weekend when the streets and stores were crowded. Bonus: You have nights and weekends back!

In the afternoon during the school year, we pick up our grandson and help with homework. A couple of days a week we take him to swim practice.

Getting up and out does not have to involve a car. Go for a walk. Bike to the grocery. Visit a friend. Do gardening. Rake leaves.

End the day: Cooking is a ritual to signal a break away from the activities of the day. The act itself is restorative. The dinner meal can become a transition point to a quieter time of the day.

Except for early morning news, the TV largely stays off in our household. It might come on in the evening but usually then only for selected shows. I might read. I might pay bills. I might watch a movie with my wife or a friend. Evening is a different time of day for a different focus.

All these activities are directed to creating new habits. As one habit leads to another activity and another, the trick is to start with the right habits to kick off the right sequence of events. I illustrate this idea in another of my books, *Retire to a Better*

You, by talking about my old exercise habits versus my new exercise habits.

In the old routine I pretty much did nothing. I sat at work. I sat at home. I ate too much and gained weight. When I gained weight, exercise became uncomfortable, so, if possible, I exercised even less. When I exercised less and gained more, I developed high blood pressure and high cholesterol. And down the path I went. And, I do mean down.

When I started exercise, I started small. I couldn't do big. I walked in a swimming pool for twenty minutes two or three times a week. Walking was all I could do. After a long while I changed my activity level a little more by adding some at work: I began to park at the back of the lot and walk into the building. After a while I added a small walk at lunch. That small walk eventually turned into a mile.

As I did these things, I became more *able* to do them. I felt better about them. I felt better about me. I ate better and slept better. I was able to do more at home. And so it went. This time in a positive direction.

Author Charles Duhigg talks of these patterns as keystone habits. I think these patterns are often marked by a single phrase, but really point to a series of things. For example, the keystone habit or single phrase for me was "Sit." But it really pointed to a whole host of opportunities to sit and a wide range of associated behaviors that resulted in or contributed to unintended consequences like eating too much.

The keystone is the rock upon which others rest. In architecture it is the central and last piece added to an arch, which locks all other stones in place and allows the arch to bear weight. But when the keystone starts to give, so does the structure.

Using brain scan studies, Duhigg noticed that an individual can't replace a set of patterns until a new keystone is in place.

The brain actually builds a new structure, which overlays the old. He points to exercise as an example of a personal keystone that triggers other, positive behaviors. Other habits are keystones, as well:

> *Studies have documented that families who habitually eat dinner together seem to raise children with better homework skills, higher grades, greater emotional control, and more confidence.*[35]

OK, kids! You heard it here. Come to dinner. Together. It wasn't an accident that I included regular meals in the suggestions for the day. Duhigg also suggests making your bed. It's not that regular, family meals cause positive effects, but the shift toward doing regular meals starts a chain reaction that helps other good habits take hold.

Eat regularly even if you are alone and don't have a family to join you. The regularity counts, not just the presence of the family.

A new boss

Notice what is happening here as we build the daily schedule. *We* are building the schedule. The schedule is not dictated by when we have to leave for work. The schedule is not created because the kids have to catch the bus for school at a certain time. We set the schedule. For ourselves. By ourselves.

We have more freedom in retirement than we did at work. It is just that simple.

Daniel Pink talks about the importance of autonomy to the employee. He cites in great detail the history of a

---

35 *The Power of Habit: Why We Do What We Do in Life and Business,* by Charles Duhigg. Copyright © 2012 by Charles Duhigg. Published by Random House.

company that has enacted what is called a Results Only Work Environment (ROWE, for short). In addition to paying employees well enough so that survival is no longer an issue, ROWE companies allow employees to make their own structure for accomplishing the work.

Their structure includes when they go to the office and when they go home. The times may vary daily to accommodate special circumstances. Their individualized schedule also considers how the work will be done and whether they need to meet with teammates and if they'll work at the office or from home.

The results Pink described were increased productivity and reduced stress:

> *[Employees] were focused on the work itself rather than on whether someone would call them a slacker for leaving… to watch a daughter's soccer game.*[36]

Why is autonomy important? Because being self-directed is how we were born. Pink claims our default setting is to be active and engaged. By and large, the institutions we end up trundling through tend to drive out these start-up directives. He says,

> *Have you ever seen a six-month-old or a three-year-old who's not curious and self-directed? … If, at age fourteen or forty-three, we're passive and inert, that's not because it's our nature. It's because something flipped our default setting.*

Sometimes, enforced schedules are necessary. You can't have an assembly line, even a modern twenty-first century assembly line, unless the teams show up to work together.

---

36 *Drive: The Surprising Truth About What Motivates Us*, by Daniel H. Pink. Copyright © 2009 by Daniel H. Pink. Published by Penguin Group.

And the folks down the line will fail in their task if the team upstream from them decides to be self-directed and schedules their own break time. We can put off our inclinations for a certain level of autonomy for a while in order to work that way. The sacrifice has a level of reward, including seeing progress made. But let's not repeat doing so throughout retirement if we can avoid that.

I mentioned my wife said she did the best work of her career after she left work and the office behind and took on one major project. Her satisfaction was in large part because of autonomy. She set her own schedule, collaborated when she needed to, and figured out how to accomplish the work. The only element she didn't control was what had to be done. Fortunately, she'd helped define that before she left work.

I had the luxury of having that type of work environment over the last eleven years of my career. It was absolutely phenomenal. I came and went as I needed. I could work at home within the limits of needing to attend project meetings and collaborate with others. I accomplished good things of benefit to the company. Those years I was more productive than almost any other period in my career, and definitely more productive than when I had to report for work under a boss.

Nobody is surprised at either of these results. Are you? You can work better if you are self-directed. So, why not continue the practice into retirement? Let's turn the switch back to the default setting.

> Curiosity +
> Self-direction +
> Active +
> Engaged =
> HAPPY!!

Happiness requires a mental shift in perspective. Essentially, you need to move from seeing yourself as being a pawn to becoming a player of the game. In fact, not just any player—you are the player who calls the shots.

This change of viewpoint is not rugged individualism. We are not cowboys. It is not about self-reliance but self-direction, taking responsibility for getting to the goals and not needing to rely on orders from outside. We are very likely to collaborate with others to achieve what we want. We probably can't do all that we'd like without the skills or resources of others. But we "take charge" of when and how that happens, as well.

The key to becoming autonomous is four-fold: You control

- What you do
- When you do it
- How you do it
- Who you do it with

Simple? Maybe not. When was the last time you were boss?

The secret to doing these four things is to get started early in your retirement. That's why I emphasize defining a structure as a keystone to your behavior. Remind yourself often that tackling the keystones is top on the agenda.

If you do define your own structure, the what, when, how, and who of life, a lot of great things will happen. You'll be more curious. You'll feel more in charge. You'll probably be more active than even the well-wishers who didn't want you to be bored could have imagined. And, you'll be more engaged.

On the other hand, nature abhors a vacuum. If you don't set a structure, the universe will supply one. The pajamas may even stay on until you hit the off button on the remote at the end of the day. Or, you'll get dressed and check your email. You'll snack. The mail carrier's truck might rouse you in the afternoon to get up and check the mail. The dinner bell might toll with a sound from your tummy or, if you're lucky, someone else will cook and call you for dinner.

And, you'll go to bed with a vague unease about the worth of the day or even the worth of the week. After a time you'll begin to wonder why anybody thought retirement was a good thing, let alone the grand adventure you hoped for.

But if you embrace being a player, retirement is a dream come true. You are in charge! To guarantee a good result, you have to be in charge. The old boss is on permanent walkabout. *You* have to be the boss.

Targets and goals

So, don't worry if your initial scheduling efforts need to be changed. You have to start somewhere. We are suggesting you begin by examining who you are and setting a structure intentionally. These are your targets.

We've also talked about the importance of another set of targets: the keystone habits. You need to invest heavily in two of them, particularly at the beginning of your retirement: developing your social network and taking care of yourself.

Your social network will carry you through your retirement. It is not just about having friends; it is also about having an attitude of friendliness. It is about deep friendships, as well as movie buddies. It is about sharing your life, giving benefit to others as well as receiving it for yourself. *Retire to Great Friendships: How to Grow Your Network of Fun and Support,*[37] which is a companion book to this one, provides insights and direction.

---

37 More information about the series is available at Retire-To.com.

A third companion volume, *Retire to a Better You: How to Be Able for the Rest of Your Life,* focuses on your physical well-being. Not only is the book about exercise and nutrition but also about having the character and energy to make the effort for the long haul.

Structure, an attitude of friendliness, and a character bent toward wellness will provide a solid platform after you leave work. You need all three keystones to make your retirement great.

The first step in being the boss is establishing a direction. The second is breaking that down into manageable steps. For me, setting SMART goals is the easiest way to move forward.

Direction will change. At the outset of retirement you are more focused on what the landscape looks like. As a result you'll be working on a new daily routine. You'll figure out how and when exercise fits into the day and set up new routines to cover the basics like regular meals and adequate sleep. Being at home may add to the challenge.

If you experience loss because of the transition, establish quiet time. Even if you don't

SMART

SMART is an acronym for a goal-setting process that begins with a Specific objective that is Measurable, Attainable, Relevant, and Time-bound. See more on SMART goals in Appendix C.

experience loss, quiet time may also be just the thing to help with transitioning out of the tasks and goals and objectives and deadlines of work and into something new.

Quiet time does not need to be empty. You could visit a park or garden. Take a bicycle ride or a walk. See a museum or exhibit. Don't be rushed by the need to get back to something. Allow yourself time off.

Meditating or following another spiritual discipline is a great quiet-time investment. Meander is a good word for these reflections. Watch the trail ahead. Take a different path. Just let time be with you. Relinquish demands. Just breathe.

Add these quiet moments to meals with friends. Card games. Parties. Taking a trip.

Later in retirement, the areas you want to explore or follow may be different. You may want to volunteer. You may have a part-time job. Grandchild care may need scheduling.

SMART goals can play a definite role in all of these activities. Here is a sample:

> Tomorrow I'll call my friend from across the street to go for a walk this week.

This goal is

- **Specific**: I'll make a call
- **Measurable**: Only one call is needed. Did I or didn't I follow through?
- **Attainable**: I didn't think I'd do 100 calls. Just one. I should make that OK.
- **Relevant**: I want to be outside and I want to deepen friendships. This goal relates to both.
- **Time-bound**: Day after tomorrow is too late!

How about another?

> This week I'll make the bed at least five times.

This goal is

- **Specific**: Making a bed has pretty clearly defined steps and results.
- **Measurable**: Five out of seven days is measurable. I could even make the bed five times on the seventh day! It is still measurable.

- **Attainable**: I'm used to doing it a few times a week. Adding the extra seems doable.
- **Relevant**: I heard this simple task is a key to happiness. Personally, I have to admit that now, when I make the bed, I get a kick out of it just because making the bed seems such an off-the-wall suggestion, but it certainly can't hurt. I'll try it.
- **Time-bound**: I have to do it in a week. That's a definite timeframe.

Human beings are wired for progress. We feel better when we can see results. This goes back to what I said earlier about motivation.

SMART goals clearly help with that because they make progress easily detected. I did my goals. Good.

For You

I've included a more lengthy explanation of SMART goals in Appendix C as well as some samples. You can also find more details on SMART goals and more SMART goal samples at this book's website resource page:

www.retireto.info/goforward/bookresources/

Where to

We've talked about the importance of starting retirement the right way—establishing a new structure that includes positive habits like exercise, play, and friends. We've also talked about avoiding mistakes. Opening doors to more things you can do is easy. The hard part is deciding which doors are the most *meaningful* to you.

Why Get Out of Bed

Just how do you define meaningful? Well, isn't that just the $64,000 question?[38]

I think meaningful is as meaningful does. If something makes that much difference to us, we'll go after it. We'll spend

---

38 $550,000 in 2013 dollars, according to dollartimes.com.

money on it. We'll get out of bed to do it. We'll do it instead of other things. And, when we get back into bed at day's end, we feel we've used our time wisely.

My friend Ted Klontz, who has a doctorate in psychology, told me that he has found the following to be universal needs and, as such, more significant than the merely important things in our lives:

- Belonging
- Autonomy
- Safety or security
- Self-expression
- Purpose or significance
- Connection

Psychologist Abraham Maslow projected a hierarchy of needs back in 1943. At the bottom of the list were physiological needs, just under safety. Love or belonging was above that, and esteem was close to the top. At the very top of the hierarchy was what Maslow called self-actualization.[39]

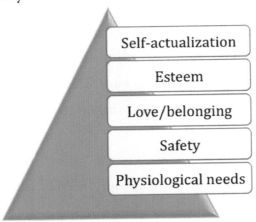

---

39 "A Theory of Human Motivation," by Abraham Maslow, *Psychological Review*, 1943. See also *Motivation and Personality*, by Abraham Maslow. Published by Harper and Row, 1954.

While the presence of these in a person's life is important, Maslow went on to say their absence is also life-shaping. A lack of food or water trumps everything else, for example. Similarly, esteem—including confidence and respect as well as morality and creativity—is not a focus if you are missing love or lack a sense of belonging.

Please note that few of these elements involve money or reward. Incentives may get some folks doing repetitive tasks to achieve more. But will a monetary reward get you out of bed in the morning? Now, if something else were at stake, such as the welfare of your family, out of bed you'd pop.

But in fact, "what is in it for me" is almost the lowest motivator in the stack. Adam Grant, an associate professor at The Wharton School at the University of Pennsylvania, reported on a series of experiments that demonstrated outcomes benefiting others are often more motivating than outcomes benefiting the individual.

- Signs that announced "Hand hygiene prevents *patients* from catching diseases" resulted in healthcare workers washing their hands more often than signs saying, "Hand hygiene prevents *you* from catching diseases."
- Lifeguards who spent five minutes reading articles about actual lifeguard rescues worked more hours, volunteered to work more often, and did things not in their job description to improve pool safety. Their performance was measurably higher than before they read the articles and higher than a control group who read articles about how being a lifeguard was beneficial to school or job prospects.
- Telemarketers for a university fundraising campaign who spent five minutes talking to a scholarship recipient (a beneficiary of the funds raised), improved their

call rates and the amount raised over other telemarketers who did not do these interviews.

- Radiologists became more attentive to detail and had higher accuracy rates just by seeing a picture of the patient along with the X-ray. This study compared new results against results reported six months earlier. The same X-rays were evaluated both times but the picture was added the second time. (Who remembers X-ray details after six months?)

- Employees who contributed to an emergency fund beneficial to other workers were more motivated than the recipients of the funds. The employers had hoped otherwise. They did the study because they thought work of the employees in need would improve if the need were removed or they felt supported by their co-workers. What they found was that it was the altruistic workers who got a morale boost; *their* performance improved.[40]

You have three ways to look at this list. The first has to do with **who** you are doing things for. The second has to do with **how** you get paid. And, the third is a question of what is of **value** to you.

The **who** answer is clear even though it may be surprising. When you focus on benefiting others, you achieve better results for yourself. There's a retirement surprise for you: Altruism is good for you!

> *As the data accumulate, it is becoming more and more evident that people who reach out to others during retirement experience greater well-being than those who do not.*[41]

---

40 "Philanthropy and Fundraisers' Motivation," Stanford Graduate School of Business, Center for Social Innovation podcast available online at csi.gsb.stanford.edu, December 21, 2010. Most of the Adam Grant studies reported here are presented in this podcast.

41 *Purpose and Power in Retirement: New Opportunities for Meaning and Significance*, by Harold G. Koenig, M.D. Copyright © 2002 by Harold G. Koenig. Published by Templeton Foundation Press.

Getting paid for what you do may not be important. You do, however, want to pay attention to **how** you get paid. Maybe it would be clearer if we talk about the kind of currency you receive. Money may not do it. Let's put this idea a different way:

> *Fifty years of behavioral science shows that contingent pay schemes—if you do this, then you get that—are effective for simple, routine work, but not very effective at all for complex, creative, conceptual work.*[42]

In fact, performance-related pay may actually decrease performance:

> *We find that financial incentives may indeed reduce intrinsic motivation and diminish ethical or other reasons for complying with workplace social norms such as fairness. As a consequence, the provision of incentives can result in a negative impact on overall performance.*[43]

(If it weren't for that last little bit about actually reducing motivation, I'd feel honored to take any bonus you wanted to send my way for writing this book! You can still send money, just please don't expect me to write faster.)

People need to be motivated not by outside incentives, but by their interest or enjoyment in the task itself. The **how** of the equation is intrinsically from *within* rather than extrinsically from what's in a pay envelope.

If you are exercising, intrinsic motivations would include your desire to feel better. No one can give you that result. You are not getting paid to exercise. Finding enjoyment being

---

42 *The Flip Manifesto: Counterintuitive Ideas About Motivation, Innovation, and Leadership,* by Daniel H. Pink. Copyright © 2012 by Daniel H. Pink. Published by Daniel Pink. Available through Amazon web services: http://danpink.s3.amazonaws.com/FLIP-Manifesto.pdf.
43 "When Performance-related Pay Backfires," a report of an interview with Dr. Bernd Irlenbusch on the London School of Economics and Political Science web page, updated May, 2011. www.lse.ac.uk.

with a friend is another example. Your friend does not supply the enjoyment; you experience it together. You don't get paid a bonus for each friend you spend time with.

Intrinsic motivation entices people to undertake tasks that:

- **Provide a challenge**: Nobody thought I could do that; so I did it anyway.
- **Pique interest**: Who knew that was hidden under there?
- **Find a solution**: A puzzle is engaging.
- **Are satisfying**: I've always wanted to do that. I've always wanted to be able to do that.
- **Improve the world**: I think this book will make a difference; I want people to experience fulfillment in their lives. Or, as Steve Jobs said: "We're here to put a dent in the universe."

The challenge, interest, search, and belief provide the motivation. To be sure, external rewards may come later for having done these things, but the motivation is internal.

That does not mean that getting paid is not significant. It may be very significant. After all, even Maslow recognized that you had to eat! In fact, you can't pay attention to other things if you are starving.

But if you enjoyed your work, the job you did for pay, chances are it wasn't because of the paycheck. The enjoyment came from within you. You found a challenge or interest or other internal motivation.

What you **value** is your choice among the options. You may like a challenge. I may prefer a task that is directed to improving the world. (I chose to improve it by writing a book that can help you!)

Intrinsic motives provide an excellent weathervane to

determine just how you would rank one retirement activity over another. Chances are your choice feels special:

> *It's that pursuit, goal, or activity that you feel like you were "meant" to do, something you could do all day, every day, for no pay and not feel tired at day's end.*[44]

Keep in mind this thing you were "meant" to do does *not* have to be the thing you do forever. It does not have to consume your entire waking existence. It does not have to define your entire being for all eternity. It does not have to be the thing you spent a lifetime to find.

Whew. Give yourself a break!

Get up in the morning and do something that sounds good. Maybe figure out what that will be the day before. Do something else tomorrow or next week. Remember, you are playing!

Now, if what you decide to do is what you were meant to do, *ka ching!* Double jackpot. Bonus time.

In *The Flip Manifesto*, a book on leadership, motivation and innovation, Daniel Pink asks several questions that can help you identify which rocks to look under to find the good stuff:

- What did you do last Saturday for fun?
- What did you do last Saturday for yourself?
- What are you great at?
- What comes easily for you?
- What amazes your friends so that they want you to do it for them?
- What would you do for free?

---

44 *How to Make the Rest of Your Life the Best of Your Life*, by Mark Victor Hansen and Art Linkletter. Copyright © 2006 by Hansen & Hansen and Art Linkletter. Published by Thomas Nelson.

I would add a couple of other search strategies to the list:

- What haven't you done in a long time that you used to really enjoy?
- What are your friends doing that looks intriguing?
- Do you have a hobby you'd like to spend more time doing?
- Did you have a childhood dream you've ignored?

Maybe you could look for opposites. My friend Duane went from being an executive to gardening, and my friend Ron went from preaching to cabinet making. They both decided to do things with more immediate and tangible rewards compared with careers of long-term and intangible or hard-to measure results.

Let's try a few other opposites:

- If you worked indoors, maybe an outdoor pursuit is in order.
- If you provided brain effort, maybe you can consider manual effort.
- If your work kept you in constant contact with inventory, something that focuses on people might be what appeals.
- As a fireman you faced danger regularly. Maybe something more sedate?

Or vice versa in each case. How would you describe some task, job, or avocation that contrasts sharply with what you've done in the past? And, please, if all things are equal and you're choosing between a passive activity and an active one, pick the active one. Gardening, and even cooking, beats watching food shows on TV. Even if you do them both sitting down, playing board games with your grandchildren is better than a solitary computer game.

Blogger Nancy Collamer has posted several ideas she's collected from different people:

- What did you love to focus on, think about, and explore when you were between age 13 and 20? (From Kathy Caprino). She thinks this exercise will help you uncover forgotten passions.

- If you were free from all the things that limit you and hold you back, in what direction would you go? (From Linsey Levine). When we remove limiting beliefs, we may uncover some golden nuggets of possibility.

- What can you do most easily when you are tired or exhausted? (From Lynn Berger). Our strengths may rest on something we've mastered but, perhaps, not recognized its value to us.

- Where does your vision take you? What locale? What kind of people? What type of place? (From Linda Van Valkenbergh). Collamer reminds us that visualization can be a powerful tool. [45]

All these people are career coaches. Their advice to the seekers of work is also good for the seekers of activity. After all, what they and we have in common is the search to find meaning, purpose, and connection. In general, go for:

- Something you find worth doing
- Something that makes a difference to the greater good
- Something that makes you feel part of a community

Why? Because these goals have intrinsic worth. They matter. We do better work when we're working on behalf of someone else. So, even if you don't want to stick with a particular activity for very long, you will have made a difference.

---

45 "How to Discover Your Career 'Passion,'" by Nancy Collamer, October 1, 2012, at nextavenue.org.

Many of us also want to find a renewed sense of belonging. The rewards and recognition and significance we felt at work came in part from our sense that the larger whole was working together. We were part of a community. We belonged.[46]

We talked earlier about finding purpose and meaning in our work. In this new phase of life, we need to find a way to replace work with new sources of purpose and meaning. Why? Because purpose and meaning are key to a vibrant, fulfilling, and empowering life. And because working as part of a community to make a difference is rewarding.

Now all you have to do is pick. You're not limited to one thing or place. You're not limited to staying with one thing. You can do more than one. You can do one and move on to another later. My wife would say choose the ones that energize you. The quotation from Howard Thurman is framed and hangs on our wall at home.

So, just what are the options? As the saying goes, they are legion.

Creativity

Enjoy the arts

In the early twentieth century, Father Edward Joseph Flanagan was ministering to homeless men on the streets of Omaha. He developed compassion for young people. Boys Town was the result. It was founded by Father Flanagan in 1917 as a residence for boys who needed a home. Now its vision is "to save children, heal families, and strengthen communities."[47]

---

46 *The 75% Factor: Uncovering Hidden Boomer Values*, by James V. Gambone, Ph.D. and Erica Whittlinger, MBA. Copyright © 2003, 2007 by The ReFirement Group.

47 See boystown.org.

My wife was impressed by Boys Town. During a visit, Crys remarked on the gardens, the stained glass, the lovely buildings and art. She was told that Father Flanagan had said, "Beauty is a silent healer." Thus, beauty became a hallmark of the organization and the spirit behind it.

If the creative arts are your passion, realize that in creating beauty, you are also giving joy and healing to others. Your art may have a reach.

My friend Jean always liked painting, but when she retired, she went after it in a big way. She now paints regularly, exhibits her work, and belongs to a group that goes on painting outings.

> *Ask not what the world needs. Ask instead what makes you come ALIVE—and do that. Because what the world needs is more people who have come ALIVE.*
>
> —Dr. Howard Thurman

She particularly likes to paint pictures of old buildings. Not "historic" enough to be a part of a regular tourist route, the buildings Jean selects are farmhouses, barns, bridges, and the like built in a bygone era. They may even be on the historic register. She combines her artistry with a sense of history and a passion for preserving its character.

Jean had been involved with painting for a long time. But Grandma Moses didn't start painting until her late 70s. Grandma became a cultural icon with her work. Her art exhibits drew record crowds. You can start something new after you retire.

You don't have to be a cultural icon. You don't have to paint. And, you don't have to be a "creative person" to be creative, either. Long hair, beads, eccentric behavior, pierced body parts, worn jeans, tattoos, denim (whatever shade is in vogue and the requisite count of holes or tears), dangling jewelry from ankles, ears or arms, and following your muse do not a creative person make.

I agree with writer and business marketing expert Michele Wacek when she says, "Creative people believe they're creative, and uncreative people believe they aren't."[48] When I taught project management classes for ten years, I made a point to tell students, "Go ahead and think you are creative. It is your only shot at it because, guaranteed, if you think you are not creative, you won't be."

When you've taken that first leap, the sky is the limit. Be playful, and

- See what it is like to mold clay or, what is it they say? "Throw a pot"?
- Pluck that banjo
- Strum a guitar
- Sing a solo
- Jam on the piano
- Write a book or some memoirs
- Redesign your flower garden
- Dance your heart out
- Act in a play
- Carve a statuette

Enjoy more than the arts

Luckily, you can be creative in many ways. I feel I'm creative when I

- Write a great sentence for this book
- Read Scripture well enough that people say they caught a new meaning

48 "Are Creative Stereotypes Holding You Back?" by Michele Pariza Wacek, blog post on Solo-E.com.

- Write or tell a story well
- Make a new photo book with a favorite set of pictures
- Figure out a set of steps to use to get my books marketed
- Sing a song better than last time
- Come up with a new spoon riff[49]

As you can see from this list, I don't believe creativity has to be limited to what is considered art. Persons with an MBA or a chemist can be just as creative as Grandma Moses. Their creativity may not be as "you can hang it on your wall" obvious. You don't have to sculpt, paint, write, act, sing, or dance. I believe a chemist has to be creative to think how his or her latest hypothesis can be tested or, for that matter, to adequately verbalize the hypothesis. Or to help a high school student understand and get excited about chemistry and learning.

Sadly, a current school of thought on creativity may hinder us from even trying to be creative. Our reluctance to accept a "creative" label may not totally be our fault. If anything, creativity itself has been put at the top of a difficult-to-attain mountain peak. We tend to think only special people can attain such rare heights.

Teacher Shelley Wright presented a concept, a taxonomy of thinking, introduced in 1956 by a group of educators chaired by educational psychologist Benjamin Bloom. Bloom and colleagues developed what I call the current pedestal view of creativity, which puts creativity at the top of an uphill struggle.

---

49 I may have mentioned I regularly sing with a band that frequents retirement and nursing homes. I may not have mentioned that the band plays gospel and country music, and I play the spoons. Hey. I live in Nashville. It's in the air!

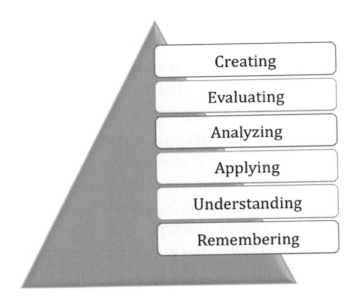

As implemented in some schools, creativity should only be introduced or attempted after the skills of remembering, understanding, applying, analyzing, and evaluating are mastered. Wright and I agree this approach has had a negative impact on the classrooms in the United States for half a century. She says,

> Teachers...spend the majority of their time in the basement of the taxonomy, never really addressing or developing the higher order thinking skills that kids need to develop. We end up with rote and boring classrooms. Rote and boring curriculum. Much of today's standardized testing rigorously tests the basement...[50]

So, basically, you and I, who attended school some time after the early 1950s, have had a lot of practice remembering and understanding but less practice evaluating and creating.

---

50 "Flipping Bloom's Taxonomy," blog post by Shelley Wright, May 15, 2012, plpnetwork.com. Donald Clark also has a blog post that explains the taxonomy well; look for the article entitled, "Bloom's Taxonomy of Learning Domains," updated last on July 5, 2010.

To hear Shelley talk of teaching "upside down" is refreshing. She starts with creativity and moves on to evaluation and analysis.

For example, she asks students to design something, say an advertisement. They move on to evaluating their mock-up against professional examples, and then to analyzing them for similarities. In that fashion they are guided to discover the design principles. When they then read about them, because of their experience, design theory takes on a depth of meaning the students probably would not have understood as readily had they come at the task in the traditional manner.

Because Shelley reports similar results teaching science concepts and grammar, I'm encouraged to take her "upside-down" approach further. What can you and I learn? How do we start with creativity?

Retirement as a creative endeavor

Retirement itself is a great example. Suppose in our retirement, we ask first what we'd like to do and worry about the implications afterward.

In our workshop entitled "The New 3Rs of Retirement," Crys and I give attendees a chance to follow the example set by our friends Foye and Carole. As they were planning for their retirement, they started with the question, "If you dreamed you had the perfect retirement, what would it look like?"

Turned out Foye and Carole each saw mountains in their vision of retirement. Soon they were on a quest to move to the place of their dreams. With their goal in mind, their problem was to figure out how they were going to make it happen. Some obstacles did stand in their way. In the economy of the past few years, selling their home, for example, took some time. But they did and made the move to a new place and new life.

The point is that they started with the creative part: What would a dream retirement look like? Then they worked hard at getting to where they wanted to be.

I'm much more likely to go about the project backwards: We started by listing things we did *not* want to do! My wife and I have often told ourselves we don't want to pack up this household and move. And, by starting at that point in the discussion, certain versions of a perfect retirement are not possible to us. We would not be in the mountains like Foye and Carole.

Psychology professor Laura Carstensen suggests you and I begin to

> think creatively about ways that an unprecedented number of mature, talented, healthy adults can address society's great challenges.[51]

Her invitation starts with creativity. It invites creative responses, new ways to think about the possibilities in retirement. Want to do some political organizing? Need to start a new think tank? What if a group volunteered to support a local school, fund a favorite charity, or help plan a city project? Why shouldn't this group be one you are a part of—or start? Why not you? You are among the "unprecedented number."

I have a friend Dave in Decatur, Alabama. His church adopted a local elementary school. They decided, as a church, they could make a bigger difference if more people were involved, so they have 35 people signed up. These people plus volunteers from other churches work one-on-one with first-grade students to improve reading. Every student is different,

---

51 "A Resolution of a Lifetime," by Laura Carstensen, *AARP Bulletin*, January 1, 2012.

so they have to start with each student's particular need and work on that. And the needs are complex. They call for creative responses.

The school they chose had one of the poorest reading test results in the district. This problem was complicated by the fact that English (and sometimes Spanish) was not a primary language in many cases. Eighty percent of the kids were identified as Hispanic, but many of those had primary languages from small hill tribes in their country of origin. Parents were only able to give minimal help with the reading deficiencies.

The school reported, even in the first year, the volunteer program made a remarkable improvement in first-grade reading levels. Retirees made a difference to not only the success of the program but also to the lives of the children.

Our friend Larry spends part of his year in Florida where he works with the guys in his church to build "trikes." These vehicles give mobility to people in developing countries who've lost a limb. Mobility changes the lives of the recipients, who are then also better able to contribute to their family's well-being. As a group, Larry's friends leverage a small number of tools and small space into a much larger result. Also, others from the church can be involved, supporting the trike-builders through parts-procurement and financing.[52]

Groups. Think about it. Bring more people together for bigger results. Usually, all they need is a catalyst. Hmmm. Feel like a little chemistry? The effort may just take off—if you started stirring the pot.

---

52 Check out these two sites: His Wheels International at hiswheel.org/global-trikes and the Hand Powered Tricycle Project at thecollaboratoryonline.org.

Volunteering

While illustrative of collaborative effort, those two stories also demonstrated two of the thousands of ways you can volunteer.

My wife, Crys, volunteers for Saddle Up!, a therapeutic riding program for children with disabilities. During lessons with children, she either leads the horse or walks alongside to assist the child. Sometimes, a child will need physical support. Other times, encouragement. She is part of a well-trained team that has learned to coordinate their efforts to make the children stronger and more confident while having a good time.

Other times, Crys works with one of the horses. Because these horses are ridden by a variety of riders with a huge range of abilities and disabilities, a therapeutic horse needs the regular weekly support of an experienced rider who can bring a consistent pattern to its life. She conditions the horse.

My wife has always had a passion for riding, and this work gives her the benefit of continued connection with her beloved horses. She and I have both benefited from the training about disabilities given by the organization. The Saddle Up! program and staff are very supportive and appreciative of their many volunteers, as well as of the children and their families. Given her skills and interests, Crys has found a great community and a way to give aid to someone who benefits.

I spend part of most Sunday afternoons each month singing at nursing homes around the city. The band does gospel music primarily, and residents can sing along. Some even dance! Our group has four very consistent guys, but we offer the opportunity to many friends who are also players and singers. Because we perform from a well-rehearsed song list, the leads are solid so additional musicians have no problem joining in. Eleven was the recorded high count in the group we had one Sunday.

As a bonus, we combine our volunteer work with other goals. Some of us in the band get together after a performance to have a bite to eat. With service to others we add an opportunity for deepening our social connections.

Our friend Marcia's sister volunteers for two different groups four days a week. Not only is she helping others, but also she's meeting new people and has gained the structure she felt she needed after retiring.

High on our list of favorite volunteers is Gordon. Gordon was a docent for the cathedral in Yorkshire, England. We accepted his offer to show us around Yorkshire and had an absolutely amazing time. We could not have hired as good a guide.

Gordon refused a tip because he found this activity a way of giving back for the hospitality he had received in World War II. He was a soldier stationed in Canada and appreciated his home away from home. Thank you, Gordon.

Finding volunteer activities

Volunteering opens up lots of opportunities to re-invest, and finding them is not difficult.

- **Volunteer Match** (volunteermatch.org): The folks at Volunteer Match have literally thousands of sites recorded in their database of opportunities all over the U.S. On a whim, I entered Boston, Massachusetts, with the key words "meal" and "delivery" and found a position for a Meals-on-Wheels driver.
- **AARP** (aarp.org): Similarly, AARP now has a new tab on their website for volunteers. It has articles of interest to

volunteers, including information about opportunities. The site also highlights a "volunteer wizard" that guides you through a series of questions to help you find a good match. It starts with skills, asks about the target age of people you'd like to help, how often you can help and when and, finally, where you'd like to do the helping.

- **Senior Corp** (seniorcorps.gov): Senior Corps connects people 55+ with service opportunities. They ask you to join the organization. They have three programs. The Foster Grandparent program connects members to young people with exceptional needs. Senior Companion Program ties members to adults who need assistance with daily tasks. RSVP places volunteers in other service opportunities.

- **Hands on Network** (handsonnetwork.com): The Hands on Network can connect you to any of 250 volunteer action centers around the world, which makes it easy for many people to find volunteer opportunities close to home. In Tennessee, where I live, we have Hands on Nashville (hon.org). They are great for finding something that is a good match for you. I put in the keywords "meal" and "delivery" again and got six returns for the next week. They are also event-oriented. Local organizations can request volunteers for a specific date. So, lucky for you, if you have an opening for next Wednesday, you can see what's happening.

I'm willing to bet you could find a website or two available for volunteer activities on any activity you'd care to name. I just did a search with the key words "volunteer" and "computer" and got a whole page full with a promise of a possible 133,000,000 more, give or take.

Try your favorite. I picked a set I thought would not be found: "volunteer" and "wind surfing." I found you could help with the American Windsurfing Tour and another opportunity where you can use your Spanish. Yet another helps Girl Scouts learn to windsurf. Total Hits: 558,000!

Get the idea? Your opportunity is probably only limited by how much time you are interested in spending on the computer and how creative you are at asking the question. For the past year or so, I've stockpiled articles about volunteering just to get a flavor of what's being reported. I found people who

Plant trees	Help with Scouting programs	Coach or referee	Tutor in almost anything	Read to kids at the library or school
Act as a tour guide or docent	Write a blog	Pilot	Help build or keep an urban garden	Teach or assist a teacher
Drive a wheelchair at the airport	Do caregiving	Care for grand-children	Adopt a highway	Paint or garden for a neighbor
Build or repair a house	Make dresses for African children	Advocate for a cause	Volunteer at the symphony, theater, or sports event	Teach a class
Practice their profession for free someplace	Volunteer at a senior center	Volunteer at the VA or another hospital	Sing or play with a musical group	Help serve meals at a church or a shelter
Deliver meals to home bound	Join the Peace Corps	Teach English	Help with clothing drives	Pick up trash in a river bed
Work a benefit	Raise money	Collect clothes or other shelter items	Work with persons who have disabilities	Put your favorite here!

Volunteering is also a great way to explore the possibilities for employment. I spoke earlier about our daughter. Ultimately, the volunteer work she did helped her determine her direction in life. At Saddle Up! where Crys helps with children and horses, many of the *employees* began as volunteers—another potential side benefit of volunteering.

Finding someplace to volunteer may only be the first step. If you have a particular skill to offer, it may take a little extra work on your part to actually get to use it. For example, our friend Trish is a board member with three different non-profit organizations. She feels, as a former manager with a large health-care company, being on a board fits her skills and interests and allows her to give back.

Get on board

But there are big differences between cleaning up the flowerbeds in a park with your neighbors and being part of the park board. Let's talk about a few of the things involved in being a volunteer as a board member.

Generally, board members are recommended or sponsored. I was a member of the board of a local non-profit called Hospital Hospitality House, which offered a low-cost home-away-from-home to family members of long-term patients in local hospitals. I was recommended for the board for my computer skills by a then-current board member.

Trish is a treasurer of one of the organizations she works with and brings her management experience to help with issues of operation and policy to all three of the boards where she volunteers. Her experience illustrates the point that board members often have a particular skill to offer the mix.

In fact, some boards will target prospective board members who have skills or are known in a defined context. Trish spoke of having a landscape architect, attorneys, a financial advisor, and a partner from an accounting firm on one board with her.

Board members recognize from the outset that their skills may very well be called on during their tenure.

The skills needed by one board may not be needed by another. Trish serves on one board with oversight of research activities. Another works to provide an audit function for the organization. These organizations require different skills as well as interests.

Finally, board members are often chosen because they can potentially be a financial contributor. If you feel you can participate this way, go for it!

Generally, board members have to pass through a review or screening committee for approval and get voted onto a board for a given period. I even had an interview with the director. Committing to being on a board may take a while and will almost certainly entail a long-term relationship with the organization. I was a board member at Hospital Hospitality House for three years.

Still interested? The best bet is to talk with the executive director of the organization you want to help. Please don't go in telling the director, "I want to be in charge of your checkbook!"

Instead, expect to be asked to do some intermediate job. You might assist with a fundraiser, for example. The people in the organization will get a chance to see that you're interested and serious about helping. And, by the way, they get to meet you. That will give you an entrée.

The testing goes both ways. You get a chance to see how well the organization does things. If you're good at organizing, you may be able to contribute with suggestions that would make a difference.

So, if you have a particular interest, seek involvement by hunting for an institution rather than a volunteer role.

All these ideas are well and good, but what if you can't find a volunteer job you want. Consider the wheelchair. Our friend Carol Ann got the assistance of an attendant to transport her husband back and forth in the airport. When offered a tip, the man refused, saying that he was a volunteer.

My perception has always been that a porter was an employee who counted on tips to make ends meet. I never expected a volunteer in that role. So, if you want to do something and have an idea of where you want to work, maybe a step forward is in your future. March up to the powers-that-be and volunteer. Create your own opportunity.

What to expect as a volunteer

As with any activity, finding the job is just the first step. Organizations are growing in their recognition of a pattern to being a volunteer. Consequently, if the organization you are scouting is on top of things, it will have support and training for you along the way. This help can be defined by stages:

Do I really want to do this? Some organizations have numerous entry points where volunteers can be of assistance. Many offer opportunities for potential volunteers to see the types of activities available. Not all tasks would be of interest to everyone. These review programs are particularly helpful if it is not clear from the outside what there is to do.

New kid on the block: You should be able to have help understanding your role in the organization. This could be as simple as "the dirty dishes go here." It may also be so complex that it needs a 10-hour training cycle. When my wife applied to work with horses at Saddle Up!, they required her to demonstrate her riding ability and pass a written test. You can't get on their horses without knowing what you're doing! Good for them; ultimately, that policy protects the kids, as well as the horses.

Valued contributor: With experience, volunteers become committed to the organization, measured by how frequently they work, how long they stay, and how long they plan to stay. While recognition programs are nice, by and large, volunteer retention has to do with how well the volunteer becomes integrated into the life of the community.

> *These elements may change significantly during the period of volunteering. People may start to volunteer for certain reasons, such as a desire to help others, and continue to do so for different reasons, such as a strong affiliation with a volunteer peer group.*[53]

In other words, you can expect that your association with any one volunteer organization may have different flavors as time goes by.

Obviously, some organizations will not have a formal process for volunteer training and support. Usually, size is the determining factor. The larger the staff, the more likely volunteers will be nurtured carefully.

The corollary is that large organizations are likely to use more volunteers. If you want your volunteering to help you find people who share interests with you and to make friends, starting with a larger organization may offer more prospects. If you want to feel you're making a bigger difference, volunteer for a smaller organization. You choose: Big fish in a small pond or little fish in a big pond.

How do you know when to move on? The answer is largely up to you—it's subjective. You can use the following questions to help gauge:

---

53 "The Volunteer Stages and Transitions Model: Organizational Socialization of Volunteers," by Debbie Haski-Leventhal and David Bargal. Copyright © 2008 by The Tavistock Institute. Online version available.

- Do you like doing the work?
- Do you like the people with whom you work?
- Are you providing a service?
- Are you finding other things you would rather do?

Another reason you might want to move on has to do with how hard you are working. Don't forget play. You don't want to get sucked into traps that lead away from caring for yourself or family. Douglas Lawson, the guru of giving and volunteerism, has this advice:

Carry a card with five small phrases on it:

- *Don't overextend yourself physically.*
- *Don't overpromise.*
- *Don't try to do it all alone.*
- *Don't overreact.*
- *Do find time to enjoy your work.*[54]

If you find yourself unable to comply with these maxims, reevaluate. Is it time to move on?

I hope you *like* volunteering—because research indicates that volunteers

- Enjoy greater functional ability
- Suffer lower rates of depression
- Have more satisfaction
- Have lower mortality rates
- Experience less pain
- Have less heart disease

All of these benefits were true for volunteers 55 and older.[55]

---

54 *More Give to Live: How Giving Can Change Your Life,* by Douglas M. Lawson, Ph.D. Copyright © 1999 by ALTI Publishing.
55 "Health Benefits of Volunteering: A Review of Recent Research," by Corporation for National and Community Service, April 2007. This is a compendium of studies; while one study would target a 55 and up age range, another might target 70 and older.

Education

We mentioned intellectual stimulation as one of the positive things we have gotten from work. And we know from research that our brains need to make new connections in order to stay healthy. So education is a great way to take care of yourself as well as another way to re-invest. And education is a two-way street; you can learn and you can teach.

Learning

Last summer we had the great joy of visiting old friends from school four decades ago. One of the things we did during our visit was to take Herb up on his offer to hear a lecture he'd been looking forward to. When the presentation was over, all six of us had a great time talking about the content. Did we agree? Why so? Why not?

On the way home Crys and I agreed we had enjoyed it immensely. A lecture-and-discussion session was one of those activities we'd not spent much time on since graduate school. It was stimulating. For the most part, the discussion topic was inconsequential; nothing significant would change if we agreed with the lecturer or not. But we learned something and straightened out a couple of ideas we had held for a long time.

A new idea emerged when we got home. We looked through the Great Courses series (they sell educational DVDs on a wide range of topics) and picked one we thought would provoke discussion. We emailed neighbors and local friends we thought would be interested in joining us. Nine of us spent the next 12 weeks at our house for an hour and a half each week with *Understanding the Mysteries of Human Behavior.*

The course had 24 lessons, so after the introductory session we had the group select the topics for the remaining weeks. We tried to figure out why we dream, why we fall in and out of love, why we make mountains out of molehills, why conflict and prejudice exist, why some relationships last and others do not, and much, much more. And, we had a great time.

The group was intergenerational—ages varied from late 20s to late 70s. The education level ran from high school through Ph.D. But everybody contributed and everybody enjoyed. No topic was off limits.

At the end of the 12 weeks we had a potluck. Crys and I had to chase people away from the table after talking non-stop for four hours. We obviously made fast friends. Everyone wanted to know when we were going to start another session.

Are we going to sponsor another one of these things? You bet. This time we're proposing people recommend their favorite TED Talks.

Did we learn things? Yes, actually. As an example, in one of the companion volumes to this book, *Retire to Great Friendships*, is a footnote about how being responsive strengthens connections between people. Our 12-week discussion group made a helpful contribution to the issue of keeping long-lasting relationships.

That discussion series included quite a few things that were new experiences for us. We hadn't had that group of people together before. We had not previously met some of the people and might not have ever met them if we had not created the group. We had never heard the professor before. Only one of the participants had spent much time studying psychology, so most of us hadn't discussed the topics before. New is good.

Educational opportunities abound if you want to keep learning. You don't have to run a do-it-yourself seminar on a topic, either. For example, I understand from Crys' cousin Carmen, people over 60 in Ohio can attend college classes for free.[56]

Every year, one of our local private schools runs a night-class adult program to benefit their scholarship efforts. We get a double-header! We learn something and contribute to a good education for a child who could not otherwise afford it.

Such classes are all around you. You can find them in public schools, churches, and synagogues. Universities and community colleges love to offer them because they are a way to introduce their campuses to potential long-term students. Community centers, professional organizations, YMCAs, and other facilities offer a wide variety of courses.

You could do a class per day for the rest of your life from the Great Courses series and travel until your suitcases wore out with the Road Scholar folks. The sky is the limit in what you can learn. You can meet people, and you can have fun. All at the same time.

Why limit yourself to one-time classes? Why not get a degree? Did you finish college? Don't you want to take on that graduate program you so longed for? Maybe you could go for or finish your doctorate? What's to say you can't complete or start an educational program that you always wanted to undertake?

Then too you could change topics. I was tired of programming. So, I started a new company. I've been learning something new virtually every day since then. I've taken several classes, from marketing to titling, from writing to how to make an elevator speech. I'm reading more. Learning energizes me! I may as well have embarked on a new degree program for what I've had to learn along the way in order to write these books. I expect I'll need to do more, and I look forward to it.

---

56 The Ohio Department of Aging confirmed this on its website: aging.ohio.gov.

Our friend Robin has a great story about changing topics and going back to school. She had a successful career in medical diagnostic imaging, but needed a change. She didn't particularly have a plan for what to do. She just knew it would have to be something different.

Robin got caught in that period we discussed earlier called the fertile void. It was obvious that she didn't want the old career any longer. Figuring out what to substitute was problematic.

Along the way she explored options. When my wife met her, Robin was volunteering at Saddle Up! During this time, Robin also volunteered for the Humane Society. Are we beginning to see a pattern here? Last but not least, she volunteered at the zoo.

It wasn't a particularly big insight to Robin that she had an interest in caring for animals and she wanted to do more with them. What took a while was deciding that going to school and getting a new degree was the way to go about it. The zoo fixed that for her. Robin discovered that to work there, she needed a different degree. So, off to college she went. Again.

The zoo has also kept her occupied. She has transformed what was a volunteer position into an internship. That makes her college advisor happy and keeps Robin with the animals. And it has potential for career possibilities after graduation.

So what's holding you back?

For some, **money** may be a problem. Will continuing your education be difficult to manage financially? If you are a woman, you might check what's available for women over 55 through the AARP Foundation.[57] In general, senior citizens qualify for scholarship assistance in most universities right alongside students in any age group.[58]

---

57 "Educational Grants for Women Over 55 Years of Age," eHow.com.
58 "Financial Aid for Older and Nontraditional Students," finaid.org.

Inquire about financial aid available to local universities in your state. Maryland, for example, offers tuition waivers and other benefits to qualified residents over 60. Your best bet will be to go to the university of your choice and ask at the admissions or financial aid office.

Prior to retirement, the **time** your job required was a major barrier to your continuing your education.[59] Once you are retired, at least that barrier disappears.

Is housing an issue? Are there colleges and universities nearby? Are you considering moving to a retirement community? Before you decide to go off to college, consider this tip: search first for the academic community rather than the community based on age. Colleges and universities are sometimes sensitive to these issues and may be able to steer you to appropriate housing near campus.

Perhaps the biggest barrier to continuing education is **ageism**, which can pop up in admissions staffs, teachers, and students. But by far the biggest attitude that can get in the way is your own. "I'm too old." Whoops!

And, oddly enough some seniors reject other seniors. "I don't want to go to school with a bunch of old folks." Whoops again! This attitude of rejecting older learners is a little more prevalent in continuing education circles, where other seniors are more numerous than they probably are in a degree program. Quite the opposite, our friend Robin found that her teachers and fellow students at the university valued her life experience.

A story is going around on the Internet about Rose, an 87-year-old who went to college because she always dreamed of having a college education. "And now I'm getting one," she

---

59 "Reinvesting in the Third Age: Older Adults and Higher Education," a study funded by the MetLife Foundation on behalf of the American Council on Education, Copyright © 2007 by American Council on Education.

reportedly says. The story may be factual, or it may be an urban legend. Either way it speaks truth. The part I like is the advice she supposedly gave to attendees at a football banquet:

> *There is a huge difference between growing older and growing up.*
>
> *If you are nineteen years old and lie in bed for one full year and don't do one productive thing, you will turn twenty years old. If I am eighty-seven years old and stay in bed for a year and never do anything, I will turn eighty-eight.*
>
> *Anybody can grow older. That doesn't take any talent or ability. The idea is to grow up by always finding opportunity in change. Have no regrets.*
>
> *The elderly usually don't have regrets for what we did, but rather for things we did not do. The only people who fear death are those with regrets.*[60]

Attitude makes a difference. Let your excitement about something new, about an adventure, and about increasing your knowledge carry you forward. Negative images of whom you'll meet and what they'll be like or opinions of your own capabilities need not deter your journey.

Another major intrinsic motivator—mastery of something, even the pursuit of mastery—is energizing. Daniel Pink has identified three laws of mastery:

- **Mastery is a mindset**: This law is parallel to the creativity mindset mentioned earlier. If you don't think your intelligence can grow, you are assured of being correct; your intelligence won't grow. However, if you think

---

60 I found this story with a simple Google search on "Rose college story." Its authenticity hasn't been verified. Whether it's true or not, it delivers an important message.

your intelligence will grow, you've no guarantee of success, but it is your only shot at it. So, go for it!

- **Mastery is a pain**: This is the "true grit" story on steroids. You have to grin and bear it. Mastery takes patience and perseverance. It may take a while. I've forgotten more programming languages than I remember. Mastery of each involved the same arduous process. I understand the pain.

- **Mastery is an asymptote**: Think of diminishing returns and substitute knowledge for money in your illustration. The longer you learn, the less you learn for the same time investment. We used to talk about programming languages similarly. Say you took an intensive two-week course to get up to a reasonable speed; an investment of another two weeks would not give back the same volume of learning.

My wife and I compared notes the other day. Remember, she is the one who has been the editor for decades, still loves it, and still does it. I am a new programmer-turned-author. I talked of how energized I was to be learning all this new stuff.

She, on the other hand, couldn't point to taking in large gulps of fresh material for improving her editing skills. She keeps learning, but the rate is lower, which is not her fault—much of what she does is not new to her. However, as she steps into each project, wades around and pans through the material, she almost always finds nuggets of learning gold.

So, whether you want to continue on a known path and learn more or strike out in a new direction, continual learning is, or can be, part of the journey. Forging ahead down the road to mastery speaks to our drive for competence.

Competence requires mastery. You have to be good at something. But competence also requires an understanding of the world and some success in being able to perform in that world. In essence, competence is not only about mastery of something but also mastery *for* something.

I've not gained the competence level I need to market these books. I think I have the writing and publishing parts down, but I'm working on the marketing in earnest. So what happens when you don't have a feeling of competence in a certain endeavor?

- You give attention to other tasks.
- You give less effort to the related tasks.
- You are not as open to trying new approaches.
- You are more of a follower rather than a leader.[61]

Doesn't that sound like you could easily shoot yourself in the foot? I'm very careful these days to be sure that is not happening. When somebody suggests a new approach, I don't make a quick decision or, if I made a hasty rejection of the idea, I circle back around and ask myself why. I continue to challenge myself to the task of mastery of even the difficult parts.

Brendon Burchard, the author of these warnings, says one of the biggest stumbling blocks to continuing to learn is not realizing that you may *not want to* learn. Ask yourself: What was your reaction to the thought that "continual learning could be part of your journey" in your retirement?

- **Were you put off?** Boy, I'm done with that part of my life. I've had it with school.
- **Were you confused?** What on earth for? Why bother?
- **Did you feel stupid?** Yikes! I never could understand that stuff? It's way above my head.

---

61 *The Charge: Activating the 10 Human Drives That Make You Feel Alive,* by Brendon Burchard. Copyright © 2012 by The Burchard Group. Published by Free Press.

- **Were you annoyed?** Get a grip. I am trying to retire here. Go away.

Here are three principles to give you direction. I've used them. I find they have carried the day with past learning endeavors and will undoubtedly work to my advantage as I move toward that learn-about-marketing hurdle looming in front of me.

First, you can't hit the target if you can't see it. Why take a course on cooking if you don't want to cook? So, what is it you *want* to do? When you've figured that out, you can select the right venues and pick among coming attractions.

Second, you'll do better about learning if you learn something you like. In our example we're hopeful that you not only want to do more cooking, but also that you actually like to cook. Learning about something is easier if you pick courses parallel to your interests.

I remember an ancient video shown to aspiring teachers about motivation: Long ago and far away a young man eager to learn how to fix electronic equipment couldn't read. His teacher, who obviously didn't know anything about electronics, was able to show him what the next step was because she could read the manual! Needless to say, the young man learned to read.

Third, you will learn better and be more motivated if you are confident you can achieve mastery. I have learned a lot of things in my life. My ability to learn a new thing is easier because I've been successful at it. And, I'm not talking about book learning exclusively, either. I feel I can learn to swim better because I have gone through experiences that have improved my physical ability in other areas.

So, even if at one time you felt stupid about a given subject, you may not now. One thing that used to cause difficulty need not stand in the way of your learning everything else or even anything else. You now have a lifetime of advantage over that person who felt incapable long ago.

In fact that lifetime of advantage may be important because of perspective and experience. Some learning is not about new things but discovery of meaning in the old. You now may understand more about things just because you have more experience to tie into events.

It doesn't hurt if you have a community supporting the effort. My wife swims laps. She started a year ago and now has become stronger and has more endurance than when she started. She gives credit to the fact that she keeps at it and allows enough time to practice. But another part is due to the other people in the class, which has turned into a community of people who are working on their own goals of fitness and improvement but who are also supportive and encouraging of one another.

Give yourself some credit, as well. Nobody else is making you do this. You are in control. That fact alone is a good motivator to succeed. Crys talks about not having to be the best swimmer in the class; she focuses on the fact that she is a better swimmer than all those people *who don't show up*. Showing up is on you. Go for it. You can learn this.

As a suggestion, write a list of the ways you feel you've been successful. I bet you find levels of mastery in them. And, some of them will surprise you because you've done them for so long, you forget what a challenge they were at the beginning. But this discovery is important because feeling competent leads to feeling confident. Being confident is good.

Consider getting a coach. I talked to someone who knew about marketing books and started by learning what I could from him. The coach assisted me by giving direction; I found out what to study first, second, and so on. He helped me plan an approach. I can go on from there.

A personal coach can assist by encouraging and by dissuading. A coach can help you stay on the right path.

Teaching

Teaching is the flip side of learning. Training, coaching, and mentoring are all possibilities. Those may be volunteer positions or paid employment, full-time or part-time.

When Robin returned to college for a degree in animal husbandry, she was the oldest person in the program. And she, in effect, became the mentor to a small flock of students around her. Her role happened accidentally.

Earlier, I mentioned Crys discovered a renewed passion for mentoring; she also has had a career in editorial work. Shortly after we started our company, Retirement-U, my wife had a midnight brainstorm. Why not help high school students write better? As a result she started what she calls the EZ Writer program.[62]

Crys had to search for a way to use her skills. She learned about the Bridge program housed at a local YMCA. The Bridge works with junior and senior high youth who have shown academic and leadership potential. These students come from disadvantaged backgrounds and in most cases have the potential to become the first college graduate in their family. So she initiated a call to the Bridge staff and offered a proposal.

Crys now partners with the Bridge to teach students interested in improving their writing. She gives the students one-page writing assignments and critiques their work. All of the communication is done via email. A liaison Bridge staff member also receives all emails from and to the students.

---

62 My initials make for catchy titles sometimes.

What are your skills? How might they be invested to help someone?

Want to hear a golf story? We heard of a retired person who loved golf. He became aware that his teenage neighbor was coming home from school to spend the next few hours alone until the rest of the family returned from work.

Home alone is one of those at-risk situations for youth, which can lead to less than ideal results. Knowing this, our retiree started taking the young man golfing. I don't know if homework had to be done first. I don't know how often this happened. I don't even know first names.

What I do know is that the story illustrates how activities and passions can be combined to achieve more than one end. What you know can be significant, as well as fun!

An old high school friend of Crys' loves quilting. Suzanne started a quilting group with friends who met at their church. They widened the circle to include middle-school-age girls. Now a whole new generation is learning the art. And the women feel they've made a positive connection with a younger generation—something that doesn't happen much. The girls too value the time with their older friends and mentors.

Teach English. It is estimated that by 2050, nearly 30% of the population of the U.S. will be of Hispanic origin. Add another 9% from Asia and you have a large population who may need assistance with English.

English not a passion? Maybe you have a different skill or interest but no teaching credential. An organization called Teach for America specializes in training and supplying teachers to schools that need them. While the program may have been aimed at younger adults in its early years, you will find growing numbers of seniors at the TFA boot camp gearing up to begin teaching.[63]

---

63 "A New Vision for Retirement: Productive and Meaningful," by Marc Freedman, *Harvard Business Review*, February 25, 2013.

But, you don't have to stray far from home to find someone to teach or mentor.

Crys and I do afterschool care for our grandson, Evan, who is currently in the third grade and in the throes of multiplication and division and beginning geometry. Because Grandpa is the go-to guy for math, I've had to learn a whole new vocabulary. It has been a challenge for me to learn how math is taught these days. I am far, far away from the universe where I learned math. Besides, I may have forgotten a few things—anybody remember what a rhomboid is?

Crys and I are taking Evan for a week's vacation this summer. It is one of those Road Scholar adventures. I mentioned that earlier, but did I mention Grandma-Grandpa Camp? Grandma-Grandpa Camp happens because our grandson is off on half-day adventures during the summer and has to have some place to go the other half. We've had a great time playing in the dirt, creek-walking, biking, going to museums, and more. But this story is not just about Grandma-Grandpa Camp, it's also about Bug Camp—the other half-day.

An entomology professor at the university where our son-in-law works offers Bug Camp. The professor invites children to learn about bugs for a half a day for a week. Magnifying glasses, microscopes, bugs pinned to boards, live bugs running around. Our grandson loves it!

Now, talk about mentoring! My hat's off to that professor who leads Bug Camp for two weeks each summer. He has younger elementary students for one and older ones for another.

If we cycle back to a previous example, you could possibly mentor new volunteers to an organization or to a specific task. Having a mentor is a good way for newbies to meet others, get settled in graciously, and feel supported in their new roles. For those organizations too small to have available staff time for this effort, your willingness to mentor the newcomers will likely be helpful and appreciated.

Big Brothers Big Sisters program is known as a great mentoring organization. Also, the Corporation for National and Community Service sponsors a foster-grandparent program. Both are ways to teach what you know and keep you in touch with a younger generation.

And don't forget actual teaching. Offer one of those one-night or two-night courses that are sold to benefit scholarships or other causes. Find a Sunday school class that needs a short-term presenter or long-term leader. Become a reader for the library or for kids in the hospital.

Did I mention Grandma? Long ago and far away, Crys and I were Girl Scout leaders along with two other single moms. We averaged ten or so girls and were largely flying by the seat of our pants until Grandma came along.

We weren't doing a bad job, but Grandma made it better. It seems she had been involved in Girl Scouts all of her life. At that point she'd been in or led Girl Scouts for over 60 years. When she heard of a new troop in the church she jumped right in: "What can I do? Call me Grandma."

Because of Grandma we could proudly announce to the kids' parents that we averaged twelve years of experience per leader with Scouting. All of it was Grandma's. Grandma knew Girl Scouts. Grandma knew giving back. She was an excellent mentor to fledgling Girl Scout leaders. The girls loved having her too!

What do you know? What do you care about? What can you teach? Answers to these questions help you begin to find your place in the mentoring arena. If you are already using your skills in an organization and you'd like to kick up your participation a notch, find out what you can do to help someone else.

I encourage you to seek out the opportunity to be a mentor. It brings a lifetime of rewards and gracefulness to your life. My wife loves horses. Over the years she has worked with several people to teach them the pleasure of riding. She continues to receive pleasure in return.

Employment

My wife and I took an eight-week retirement course at a local church. Several of the people at the table were retired, like Crys. Like me then, several were not retired.

A couple of the people approaching their eligibility to retire had trouble with the idea of quitting work. They didn't want to do it. What they were doing in their jobs was still meaningful to them and they wanted to continue.

So be it. Employment is a legitimate retirement option. Sounds a bit odd. But, why not?

Some Eagles Ride

Tom, who ultimately became an Eagle Scout, got a merit badge for horseback riding with Crys' help. It was a badge no other boy in his troop had ever earned.

Crys went on to teach Tom's dad, Dave. Lynn went riding with Crys for years from the time she was ten. And Allie, a next-door neighbor, got riding lessons from Crys, as well, when she was in elementary school.

Here is the lifetime part: Dave and Tom have continued to be a part of our lives and join the rest of our family for dinner on Monday night. Allie, now off to college, is taking a riding class and always comes to see us when she's home. Lynn is half a continent away, but Crys still gets Christmas pictures and notes faithfully.

Why rock the boat? Many folks who reach retirement age walk right on by the door without giving the handle so much as a jiggle. An acquaintance of mine, Watt, will likely sell insurance until the company runs out of insurance to sell. He just likes doing it. But he also does it on his own schedule.

Then too, some folks cannot afford to quit work, which makes for a great incentive to keep doing it. According to a Gallup Poll conducted in April of 2012, fully 64% of employed U.S. workers do not think they will be able to live comfortably after retirement.[64]

This expectation translates directly into continued employment. Reporting on a U.S. Department of Labor chart from February, 2013, NPR's Ina Jaffe noted that over 35% of men between 65–69 are in the workforce today. Close to 21% of women in that age range are still working, as well.[65]

Continuing to or going back to work is an obvious choice when you think about it. If you don't want to give up all the good things about work and you don't want to face a day that has a hole where work used to be, don't. Keep working instead.

I don't think people who go back to work after retirement age are much different from my grandparents, who made a transition from the farm to town. As near as I can tell, they gave up some barn animals and the tractor. In turn they got a bigger garden. Grandpa didn't grow wheat any longer, but he had a wonderful grape arbor, cherry trees, a pear tree, and an apple tree.

For my grandparents spring was spent planning for and planting the garden. Summers meant weeding. Summers and fall meant harvesting, canning, and freezing. Everything. Pears. Peaches. Corn. Green beans. Peas. Cherries. Winter meant sharpening and cleaning tools, sewing, mending clothes and equipment. Largely self-sufficient, they seemed not to know any other way than to keep working.

---

64 "Expected Retirement Age in U.S. Up to 67," by Jeffrey M. Jones, April 27, 2012, www.gallup.com.
65 "Series Overview: More Americans Working Past Retirement Age," by Ina Jaffe, February 13, 2013, National Public Radio (npr.org).

My grandparents probably didn't think of this cycle as work. It was a way of life. I think my friends who continue to work feel the same way. No one draws a line in the sand and says when you get to it you are retired. You don't always have to quit work. The line is artificial.

I know others who use the artificial line of retirement to make a change. Retirement is the opportunity to strike out in a new direction. For them the retirement line is a starting line, not a finish line. Have an adventure, even if the adventure involves work.

One option, of course, is to take that vocation you love on the road. Make a change of venue. A new locale, goal, or audience can spice up an old favorite.

Doctors Without Borders could literally send you to Timbuktu to practice your profession as a physician. Habitat for Humanity will let you use your building experience for good folks who cannot afford to build on their own. Did you like rearing your kids? You could be a nanny and help another generation. As a retired firefighter, you might consult for a volunteer fire department, which can benefit from your training and experience. As a contractor or skilled construction worker, consider building a boat instead of a house.

My father-in-law was a good role model for a second career. When he retired, he took up a part-time job as a handyman. I use the term "part-time" loosely as what this usually meant was that he took off when he wanted. Generally, he worked a lot. How many small repairs do you need around your house that you don't know how to do, don't have time to do, or don't want to do? That's why he was in demand.

My father-in-law was a widower. We used to tease him about the keys. He had this huge key ring with an enviable collection of front-door keys—all to widows' houses. Well, maybe not all, but a lot! They needed him.

He enjoyed the work. He liked fixing things. He also fixed the toys at a daycare center and became their Santa Claus— all year long. He did countless projects for us, as well. And he helped supervise the construction of the educational wing of his church. Everybody loved Mr. Petty.

He was, without a doubt, very happy. Being a mining engineer, he was happiest working with big equipment in the mine. He did not like managing mine operations. So for him, keeping his hands dirty with plumbing repair, roof vents, making cabinets, and a paint job here or there was just fine.

He went back to work. How many times have you heard of a retired person doing that?

My friend Ted has retired twice so far and is working on his third career. Steve is our current handyman and a former vice-president of human resources. My friend John "keeps his hand in" by keeping the books for the company he retired from. Let's not forget me; I am writing books instead of programming. Crys is still editing.

Jim talks of collecting portfolios. Unlike me, I don't believe he's left things behind; he keeps accumulating expertise, skills, interests, professional acquaintances and all the other trappings of a new career.

In fact Jim thinks the word *retire* should be retired. He says it was an artificial name assigned to a set of people who no longer need to exist. During the Depression, when the country was anxious to get young men off the streets and into jobs, moving "retirees" out of their way was important. That was a long time ago.

Even after the Social Security system was enacted, retirement didn't happen overnight. It took decades before the concept caught on because the people being moved out were resistant to losing the jobs that gave them meaning. It also took decades for pension and investment programs to grow to where many felt they could afford to retire.

Seeing the concept of retirement as not only moot but also derogatory, Jim is not the only one to feel the word *retire* has passed its usefulness. Blogger Mel P. believes

> *[Retirement] is nothing more than a deceptively packaged form of age discrimination that propagates the notion that older people should withdraw from productive roles in society. It fosters the perception that older people are a burden to society.*[66]

These days a lot of folks look forward to retirement whether they have a pension plan in place or not. It doesn't matter whether the notion of retirement is age discrimination or not. It does matter that millions of people now buy into the idea of retirement and look forward to the change. It is also true that many of them will ultimately be employed again.

So, if you find you have to work or you just want to work, do something wild and crazy this time. Play a little. Find a job that really makes you feel good about getting out of bed. Maybe you could find a new job or career that is interesting. Maybe find one that gives back. Maybe you can recapture that long lost feeling of adventure you had as a child or youth by doing…

Exactly. What shall you and, for that matter, I do? Where shall we look?

Career coach Nancy Collamer says the options to do flexible and entrepreneurial work have blossomed just in the past ten years because:

[66] "Time to Retire the Concept of Retirement," by Mel P., a blog post from *The Next Hill: Rest Stop for People Starting Something New*. October 13, 2009. www.thenexthill.com.

- **Technology has completely revolutionized how, where, and when we work.** Your garden or back porch can become your new office.
- **The options for flexible employment have improved and diversified.** Work-from-home possibilities have increased.
- **The costs of running your own business have decreased.** You don't have to have a storefront to sell goods or services.
- **The global reach of the Internet has made it possible to sell to anyone, anytime, anywhere.** Look for our forthcoming online course version of the Retire To message; it will be available soon right on your computer screen!
- **Freelance has become the mantra of the folks supplying services to the outsourcing business world.** I have one contractor working on workbooks and another editing. They love working from home. I love not having to supply a workplace.
- **The Internet gives us access to information and training 24/7.** You can find videos, courses, associations or experts on a huge range of topics. It may be a joke at our Monday night meal about how many phones pop into use when a question is asked, but the truth is that, if the Internet were not available, we would not be able to do a lot of things easily.[67]

Collamer's book is worth a look because she interviews people going about their second-career jobs. By all accounts, they're having a ball doing them. The starting place for your exploration, then, is to find out what others are doing.

---

67 *Second-act-careers: 50+ Ways to Profit From Your Passions During Semi-retirement*, by Nancy Collamer, MS. Copyright © 2013 by Nancy Collamer. Published by Ten Speed Press.

Here are a few more resources I recommend:

The **Encore Career**[68] folks see a second career in order for many. They point to a variety of helpful resources in their book called the *Encore Career Handbook.* I found the self-assessment tool that examines motivation options very helpful. Why do you want an encore career?

> *"Don't aspire to make a living. Aspire to make a difference."*
>
> — Quoted by Denzel Washington from an unknown author

- For health insurance?
- To continue to learn?
- For a change of scenery?
- To be your own boss?
- To feel fulfilled?[69]

These are a few of the choices shown. I like the Encore group's approach because they promote second careers for the greater good. Giving back. It is fun to watch their contest every year and see what others are doing. Creative. Beneficial. Interesting. The diversity is amazing. The ambition is exhilarating. The vision is astounding. It just may be a motivational jumpstart.

NextAvenue: Sponsored by PBS, this website is a repository of articles, videos, and interviews about a range of relevant topics like health, caregiving, money, and our current topic, work. Subscribe to their newsletter for a while and benefit from the range of information they make available.

SecondAct: Even though it is sponsored by *Entrepreneur* magazine, the website has a broad range of topics you might

---

68 Encore.org.

69 *Encore Career Handbook: How to Make a Living and a Difference in the Second Half of Life,* by Marci Alboher. Copyright © 2013 by Civic Ventures. Published by Workman Publishing, Inc.

not expect. In the "Health and Fitness" section, for example, you can find stories about people changing careers into health or fitness related fields. But you can also find health and fitness related articles, links, and stories.

The "Giving Back" section is inviting with its success stories. It is also helpful with posts offering tips for your transformation into the non-profit world. Need some tools to become a social entrepreneur? Find them here.

LinkedIn: Many of you may already know of LinkedIn as a business-oriented social network. With LinkedIn you can join a group and pursue an interest. You can find out what's interesting to people in a given field and what they talk about these days. You can engage with these folks at will. Your participation level with LinkedIn is at your discretion. Offer articles, join chats, or just watch and listen.

My Next Move: This website provides an online, interactive tool to assess personal interests and work experience. These facts are used to identify opportunities tailored to you. Sponsored by the U.S. Department of Labor/Employment and Training Administration, this site gives you three ways to search: keywords, industry, or what you like to do.[70]

Apprenticeship: Want to kickstart a second career with actual experience? You might want to check out the possibility of becoming an apprentice. While many apprenticeship programs are available to snag younger employees, many may be open to you, as well.

If you've just started receiving Social Security, chances are you cannot earn over a certain amount without having to return part of your benefit check. Some employers have learned they can pay that amount and get an experienced employee to boot. So, how much do you need to earn?

---

70 mynextmove.org. Take a look also at myskillsmyfuture.org.

Strength Finder: To counter the fact that people often devote more time to fixing shortcomings than developing strengths, the Gallup organization launched a new approach in 2001 by offering an assessment tool that starts with strengths.[71] In 2004 their research demonstrated that this approach pays off. They found that by focusing on strengths, the chances of becoming disengaged go way down: to the 1% level. Focus on weakness, and disengagement jumps to 22%.

> *Retirement is a starting line.*

Resources may also pop up near where you live. I came across a website entitled "Discovering What's Next," which offers services to the Newton, Massachusetts, community. Their mission is helping folks find meaningful encore careers. The nice thing about *local* organizations is that they can offer in-person services, events, workshops, and community.

In this search, remember the mantra: Retirement is a starting line.

Caregiving

Sometimes caregiving is thrust into our lives. As parents age or a spouse becomes ill or life takes a downward slide for someone you love, you may be unceremoniously ushered into a new role. We are of an age when we will see those we love declining.

As ability is the first loss in a sequence, care may be needed. Sometimes, the cosmic arrow for giving it points to you.

I'd love to be able to tell you what to do when the arrow does point your way. But, in a book this small, I can only scratch the surface of such a large topic. Besides, I'm not an expert. So, what I will relate are the experiences I've had in several areas: hospital care, care at home, and hospice.

---

71 *Strengths Finder 2.0: Now, Discover Your Strengths,* by Tom Rath. Copyright © 2007 by The Gallup Organization. Published by Gallup Press.

Hospital care

First, *extended* hospital care is a rarity. If extended care is needed, other facilities specialize in those areas. I've visited many knee and hip replacement customers at the rehab center. After surgeries, patients are often moved to an intermediate-care facility before going home.

Whatever rehabilitation these organizations provide, occupational therapy is almost always among them. Treatment often includes physical therapy for strength and flexibility, as well. The goal is to be sure patients are able to cope with the routine tasks of caring for themselves at home.

When my mother became ill, I knew nothing of these procedures and, consequently, had no idea what I was getting into. The next six weeks were challenging—particularly as I was still working and she was 500 miles away. Almost ten years ago I wrote an article about the experience to help me sort out my feelings and the lessons I learned during those six weeks. In the hope that "forewarned is forearmed," I'm sharing a few of these notes. Here are summaries of four guidelines I wrote at the time:

Prepare for confusion: With general practitioners, oncologists, and pulmonary specialists reviewing charts and requesting tests and procedures any time of the day or night, the hospital experience was a jumble. Who asked for that? What for? Was the test really needed? I often only found out a test had been ordered when a tech showed up to do it. He or she had no answer for why it was ordered. The confusion was at times overwhelming.

Find a nurse: As caregivers, my niece and I never knew when the doctor was coming. It was very easy to miss the doctor's visit.

However, I found a nurse in the oncologist's practice who was able to follow Mom's case on my behalf and tell me what was happening when I called from home 500 miles away. I relied on her to be my early warning system to help me know when I needed to schedule the next trip to the hospital.

At the hospital I found one nurse I could call on because she was the keeper of Mom's casebook. I could not see inside the book, but I could find out from her which doctor to ask about notes that had been made.

Keep notes: You may be the only contact doctors have to understand the history or progression of the disease. I noted what I knew of when Mom's symptoms started and how they had progressed. I noted major tests and treatments and results, good and bad. Consequently, I was able to relay this information succinctly when needed.

Doctors take vacation or rotate weeks with their partners who, then, also have to be briefed. The hospice contact was also appreciative of my notes. She said my report gave her cause to admit Mom without requiring a more lengthy investigation on her part.

Have some support: Support for you during this time is vital. While I was staying near the hospital, I called my wife every morning. She was my lifeline. She listened while I railed against hospitals and aired my confusion and frustration. My feelings ran the gauntlet. And she listened. My niece also came to support Mom much of the time I was not able to be with her. Mom also had a great friend who was by her side every day. This "committee" was vital not only to Mom, but also to each of us.

Care at home

"In the unlikely event…" How many times have you have boarded a plane and heard that phrase and the instructions that follow? You've been told *you* are supposed to put your oxygen mask on first. The situation I've just illustrated speaks exactly to that point: Take care of yourself, so you can take care of those you love.

With an estimated 66 million caregivers in the United States alone, the need to understand what is required of you as a caregiver and how to care for yourself in the midst of it all has never been greater. That figure comes from the National Alliance for Caregiving, which represents fifty national organizations focused on family caregiving. This organization reports that 11 million (17%) of these caregivers are retired.

The caregiving role gets even more complicated when the caregiver is "sandwiched" between caring for an aging parent and a child who is not financially independent. Kathleen Bogloea, director for the Family Caregiver Support Program, which is in partnership with the Alzheimer's Association, notes that caregivers often feel isolated, have difficulty managing time among commitments, and finding resources.[72] Things may get more dicey with all parties under one roof; keeping the peace may also become an issue.

Her recommendations for a good oxygen mask apply to caregivers in general as well as caregivers caught between age groups:

Hold regular family meetings: Divide up the various tasks for the week. Make sure everyone has a chance to work through thoughts and feelings.

Ask for assistance: Ask local area agencies that assist with aging issues, a hospital social worker, a physician, or a church for help.

---

72 "The Sandwich Generation," by Kathleen Bogolea, an article updated last on 12/31/2012 on *Today's Caregiver* website: caregiver.com.

Care for yourself:

- Make time for yourself.
- Remember to laugh.
- Be present to your marriage.
- Listen to your body.

Remember *your* oxygen mask. If you fail, others will also feel the consequences. If you need to slow down or something is wrong, talk to your physician. Taking care of yourself is crucial.

Numerous resources are available. Check out the website called Family Caregiving 101. I particularly liked the section that answered the top-ten questions, things such as how to find home care services from another state and suggestions for getting siblings involved with parents' care.

Hospice

In some cases, caregiving moves from attention to "lasting" to "leaving." The disease and complications finally progress to the point that victory is not possible. When that happens (or even before), I urge you to investigate palliative care and hospice.

My mom lived in a community with a hospice facility. When it was time, the social worker for the hospital was able to contact them and get Mom situated there. I've known other end-of-life stories where hospice provided in-home care instead, and still others where it was done in the hospital. In all cases, care for the patient was no longer focused on a cure but on support.

Well-trained hospice workers direct palliative[73] care, which gives family and friends opportunity for visits, prayer,

---

73 Palliative care provides patients with relief from the symptoms, pain, and stress of a serious illness—whatever the diagnosis. The goal is to improve quality of life for both the patient and the family. This definition was provided by the Get Palliative Care website (getpalliativecare.org).

and quiet together times. The hospice team of professionals and volunteers are also a conduit of care to the family. They offer understanding of the dying process, grief counseling, contact with local churches, and more. Hospice moves the focus from medical to emotional or psychological care.

In our case with Mom, hospice gave us time. Time enough for my sister to come up, visit, and lovingly wash Mom's hair. Enough time for my daughter and her family to come so Mom was able to play with her brand new great-grandson. All the grandchildren had time to arrive. We got to say good-bye.

A number of organizations provide hospice care. However, Medicare may only cover services to select ones. Hospital social workers will likely have that information at hand and volunteer it.

But even before you must react to a need for caregiving, think proactively about reinvesting in your family.

Giving care

What are the ways in which you are giving care to your grandchildren or nieces and nephews? What investment are you making in their lives?

I mention our family's Monday night dinner throughout this Retire-To series. It has become a symbol for Crys and me of our caring for family. We started with having a regular meal for our immediate family and grew from there.

Today we honor the tradition because it is a way of helping our daughter and her family cope with the many hectic challenges in their lives. Monday is one day they don't have to cook and clean up. They can relax with a healthy meal and good conversation. Also, our grandson gets to practice his manners and show off how he's learned to be helpful.

But one day a week is not the limit of our involvement with our daughter and family. We also provide afterschool care and limited daycare during the summer.

My grandparents provided similar support to my family. I remember fondly the life I had growing up. My sister and I walked to Grandma's house after school every day. And, after Mom and Dad came home from work and we had dinner and homework with them, my sister and I went back to Grandma's to sleep overnight and have breakfast the next morning before going to school. This arrangement allowed my parents to leave for work on time. Grandma and Grandpa were doing what they could for the family.

Our friend Lanette provides morning care for her grandson. His carpool doesn't pick him up until well after his mother has to leave to take her daughters to their school. Lanette provides some afterschool care, as well.

Crys talked with a woman who had no children of her own, but who ran "Auntie Camp" for a week every summer for her nieces and nephews. Obviously, she was reinvesting in her family—helping not only the young ones, but also her sister and her brother-in-law. Listening to her, Crys said what was most obvious was how much the "auntie" enjoyed camp too. How can you be supportive of your adult children… or your siblings… or cousins—both near and far?

A basic human need is simply to be noticed; another is to be listened to. How are you noticing, listening to, coaching, guiding your family? How are you being present with these people in their journeys?

Certainly, you can extend similar courtesies to people beyond your family. Widen your definition of family beyond the biological to include those persons you have "chosen" as family. Growing up, Crys complained she didn't have a sister; her mother told her she could pick one. So she did! Crys and her chosen sister, Emma, have cared for each other for over 60 years.

Monday night dinner at our house includes not only our biological family but also "family" we have chosen—people we care about. We are the richer for having them in our lives.

Claim your role as "elder," as one who has wisdom to share, and reinvest in your family. I do have gray hair. Maybe, I'll work on the role of sage. I'll have to think on that.

A good place for inspirational stories may be Wise Elder, a website created by Seattle-area writer and storyteller Evelyn Williams. Some stories center on wise elders she knows, some on her travels. Look for these gems. They are worth the effort.

Overlap

Every one of these areas I've presented here represents a need in society. All of these are ways to reinvest, to plant seeds, to give back.

These are not discreet divisions in life. You may find your volunteering opportunities in caregiving or education. Or your creativity may turn into employment, for example.

And, over the course of the years ahead, some of these may last only for a season—and then you can move on to something different. You may have several opportunities in more than one of these areas.

Look around at the many "doors" available to you, doors that invite you to reengage with life in new ways. Play a bit. Open several; see what's inside. Find the ones that are meaningful to you, ones that give you a sense of purpose, renewed energy, and joy. Go for it!

For You

I've not gone into great detail here about my reflections on my mother's hospital/hospice stay. I learned a lot that summer and I had the foresight to write it down. Since then, I've returned to the paper and reflected more on the experience. I wrote it as a series of tips. I still think they are helpful. You can find the whole article on the resource webpage I made for this book. Find it at

www.retireto.info/goforward/bookresources

Look for the article, "The Big Top." I reveal no names or personal information as I wrote it to be shared (as it turns out) with you.

When to

The topic of "When" has two parts. The first looks at retirement by stage. Retirement can last quite a while, so we'll break these years into different categories to examine them more closely.

A second part of "When" includes tying up some loose ends. We've talked a lot about feeling a lack of direction and of recovering from a sense of loss retirement can bring. But how might you prepare and so avoid the tough parts of the transition all together?

Retirement Stages

Usually, we don't quit work and check into the nursing home the next day. More is involved. Just what transpires between the retirement part and the nursing home?

Author Richard Gentzler says retirement divides into three parts:

> Go-go
> Slow-go
> No-go[74]

The good news is that when you reached the age of sixty-five, you can keep on truckin'. The bad news is you will not be as physically able toward the end of retirement as you were at the beginning.

Measured in terms of physical ability, these stages go something like this:

- **Go-go:** This active phase immediately following retirement can last a dozen to two dozen years. And, as we've seen, it can last long enough that even a second career is not out of the question.

- **Slow-go:** This phase is characterized by less activity, primarily because mobility is limited. This phase can still be vital, enthusiastic, and energy filled, but slower and more passive. We might favor shorter family visits over longer trips. We may not begin this stage willingly.

- **No-go:** This segment may be characterized as unable to go. Eyesight, hearing, and mobility losses may greatly limit activity outside the home. Gentzler notes that home health care services or alternative housing may be needed.

These increasing restrictions are the consequence of increased years. Declining strength, vigor, and flexibility turn once enjoyable tasks of home ownership and maintenance into drudgery. These limits, added to failing eyesight, mental or

---

74 *Aging and Ministry in the 21st Century: An Inquiry Approach,* by Richard H. Gentzler, Jr. Copyright © 2008 by Discipleship Resources. Published by Discipleship Resources.

cognitive decline, or impaired hearing will limit and eventually stop our ability to drive. Independence wanes and we begin

- Scaling down our lifestyle
- Moving into housing situations that require less care on our part
- Increasing our dependence on assistance with the simple daily tasks of bathing, food preparation, and even eating.

The borderlines between the phases of Go-go and Slow-go as well as between Slow-go and No-go—and the big demarcation at the end of the line—are all unknowns. They are dotted lines that can appear quickly or slowly. A personal injury or illness can usher in one of these phases or even make us skip a phase with very little warning. On the other hand we've all known or heard of people who are active all the way to the end.

The musical group I play in that visits nursing homes used to delight in the lady who got up to do the two-step when we sang particular songs. She was 96. One day I was talking to the social worker and mentioned I hadn't seen our dancer for a week or two; turns out the dancer attended a party one Thursday night, had a good time and did her usual two-step, but did not wake up the next morning.

If I have my choice, I want to dance the night away before the last dotted line.

I realize I may not always be as active as I am now. This three-stage system of talking about retirement gives a broad-stroke, high-level view of a possible journey that specifically focuses on the topic of activity. But being active is not the same as being energetic. Sid Kirchheimer and Gale Maleskey put it this way:

Your hair will get grayer and thinner. Your metabolism will slow down. Your reflexes will lose some sharpness. Body parts will show signs of wear and tear.

For the most part, those changes are as inevitable as death and taxes. But a decline in energy is not inevitable. In fact, there are lots of things that you can do to make sure you're raring to go even while you're reeling in the years.[75]

Doctor Daniel Amen echoes these sentiments in a more recent book that focuses on brain health: "Even though getting older is not optional, having a brain that looks and feels old is!"[76]

He goes on to list basic strategies to improve your brain and offers countless illustrations of how paying attention to the following makes a difference: measuring performance, eating well, strength-building, general health improvement, life-long learning, and social networks.

Similarly, Henry Lodge, a doctor who focuses on physical health and the ability to stay active, says: "Americans have achieved such staggering longevity that the real problem is outliving the quality of life, not running out of quantity."[77] He writes in his book, *Younger Next Year*, that he believes the fitness program he endorses can help readers maintain an active, not just energetic, lifestyle.

With his constant enthusiasm, the book's co-author, Chris Crowley, goes on to say that

Most of us can be functionally younger every year for the next five or even ten years. That sounds like

75 *Energy Forever,* by Sid Kirchheimer and Gale Maleskey and the doctors of *Prevention Magazine.* Copyright © 1997 by Rodale Press.

76 *Use Your Brain to Change Your Age,* by Daniel G. Amen, M.D. Copyright © 2012 by Daniel G. Amen, M.D. Published by Crown Publishing.

77 *Younger Next Year, Live Strong, Fit, and Sexy—Until You're 80 and Beyond,* by Chris Crowley and Henry S. Lodge, M.D. Copyright © 2007 by Chris Crowley and Henry S. Lodge. Published by Workman Publishing Company.

cruel nonsense or hype, but it's true. Limited aspects of biological aging are immutable. Like the fact that your maximum heart rate goes down a bit every year, and your skin and hair get weird. But 70 percent of what you feel as aging is optional. You do not have to go there. No joke. No exaggeration, even. There's a new, tough game out there. And, congratulations, you are eligible to play. You just have to learn how.

Over and over again, I run into articles and books that insist on the same things. There are keys to improving your well-being and to maintaining an active lifestyle. With some diligence it's often possible to make the Go-go side of this equation go a little longer.

Go-go	Slow-go	No-go

We still may be limited in what we *want* to do. For example, we may not want to keep up with a house or drive in freeway traffic. But we can go down to the gathering room and do the two-step with the band!

Let's be clear about my role in this discussion. I want to be encouraging. I want you to feel enabled to take all the steps you can to be as active as you can for as long as you can, which does *not* mean I make any judgment about you if that does not happen. I do not think of you as unsuccessful, and I hope you will do the same for me.

When it is all said and done, no one will skip the last stage. It may be very short, but cannot be avoided.

Meanwhile, what you can do is give some thought and preparation for the last stages.

In your Go-go years, preparation is still key. You can plan for the coming years. During these years immediately following retirement, visit and select alternate housing arrangements for a lifestyle that will let you forget about home maintenance. Talk to your children about your plans for the future. You could even solicit their aid.[78]

What kind of aid? Here is the starter list with very brief descriptions of conversations:

- **Complete an advanced directive:** This document stipulates the type of care you wish to receive if you are unable to give instruction to caregivers. The document usually includes provisions for or against resuscitation, tube feeding, and so forth.
- **Select a durable power of attorney:** Select the person(s) who can make financial decisions on your behalf when and if you are unable.
- **Select a health care durable power of attorney:** Select the person(s) who can make health decisions on your behalf when and if you are unable.
- **Prepay for funeral and burial arrangements:** Arrange this through a funeral home or service of your choice.
- **Make account transfer provisions:** Work with financial institutions to make your accounts readily available to your children or designated others when you die.
- **Prepare funeral or memorial service:** You can specify whether you want a service or not, pick favorite readings, music, and the like. Or, you can go ahead and outline an entire program.

In most cases official forms are involved. While the forms are needed, conversation is what is most helpful. A form

---

78 My daughter has limits. If I tease her too much, she reminds me, "Behave. Remember, I get to pick your nursing home!" Hah! I'm going to pick it early. So there.

may not make your children feel certain about the decisions they may have to make on your behalf. Having heard you talk about what you desire will help. Give your children and yourself a gift—have those discussions before you need to.

One notable source for preparing this information is called "Five Wishes." Approved as a legal document in all states, the form gives you a vehicle for making decisions and for starting family conversations. You can cross off elements you don't want and write in elements you do.[79]

Another approach is the "Family Love Letter." This company, which sells products to organize your information, recommends listing a variety of things that your executor or heirs will need to know, including:

- How to find your professional advisors
- Where your investments, insurance, and other assets are held
- What employee or retiree benefits you're entitled to
- Where to find information on trusts, citizenship, military records, or business ownership
- Your plans for a special-needs family member
- Which philanthropic organizations hold a place in your heart[80]

Why do these things in the Go-go years? *Because you can.* It is hard enough to discuss the issue of resuscitation when you can talk. Imagine what it would be like if you were so ill you could not express your wishes. Besides, you are a good role model for your children by caring for these decisions in advance.

---

79 "Five Wishes" is published on the Aging with Dignity website. Some states will accept this document only if attached to the sanctioned form; check the website for your locale. www.agingwithdignity.org.

80 The Family Love Letter is a company whose founder, Donna Pagano, specializes in "getting your house in order." Check out the booklet to guide you through this process. www.familyloveletter.com.

Pre-Go

Gentzler's categories start with Go-go. But what do we do *before* that? How about Pre-Go. This stage ahead of the retirement line in the sand focuses on preparation you can do. In this book we have discussed several preparation steps already:

- Structure your day.
- Establish keystone habits.
- Wrap up loose ends.
- Get a handle on finances.

Above all, during the beginning of your retirement get back in touch with the playful you and find new ways to recover purpose and meaning. You still have a lot of life! Retirement is no place to quit on that.

But what can we do ahead of time? What can we do to prepare for all of this before we get to the invisible line in the sand called retirement? We never got to the part where we figured out how my friend Buddy got to slip into retirement without a blink. He claims he never hesitated. He says he had no feeling of loss. No fertile void. How do you do that?

To a large extent, the amount of time you have to spend during retirement to get things realigned has to do with how much you did before retirement to shift gears. For example, in the second book of this series, *Retire to a Better You*, I will talk in detail about how I began an exercise program *before* I retired.

When I did retire, exercise was already a natural starting point for the day. Having morning exercise helped fill a gap I might have experienced about losing structure. But I had that covered.

Crys and I have always been intentional about getting out and socializing. Prior to retirement, however, we began earnest talks along these lines: "Who do you want to get to know better?" We've followed up on that list often since I've retired. It is fun engaging with new people, turning them into new friends. We're reestablishing friendships we had let slip in the busyness of the last few years of working, as well.

Before retirement, I also spent a little time trying to find what interests my work colleagues had beyond work. When I found out my friend Brandon was an astronomy hobbyist, I leaped at the chance to follow up. We still head to his man cave every so often or go out to take pictures through the telescope.

When you leave work, you not only may lose friends, you lose the built-in opportunities for getting to know people. You can miss the water cooler. If you've not had the need to find new friends in a while, you may want to check out the third book of this series, *Retire to Great Friendships*.

Plan: Which brings us back to this question—What can you do *before* you retire to help you find fulfillment after you leave the job? The first, most important step is to think ahead. Don't let the question of how you're going to spend your day catch you by surprise. If you haven't retired yet, the fact that you are reading this book is a good first step.

Crys struggled in a fertile void period. I have not. Her experience taught us a lesson. I did not want to go through what she did. Being forewarned is very helpful. She had leaped into retirement, but I had a grace period for planning. From the time she retired, we talked about my retirement and what I would do. And, because of her experience, I said very clearly I did not want to retire until I had something to retire *to*.

Here is a checklist to help you with planning:

- What will my day look like?
- Where will I put exercise?
- What activities interest me?
- What motivates me?
- What are my strengths?

Try: Step two is to try things. Set up next Saturday as your trial day. Saturday is "Retirement Day." Run the day using the schedule you planned. Then, evaluate the result. Do this for longer periods as well.

Do you have a four-day weekend coming? Try the new schedule all four days. Vacation coming up? Use the new schedule for the entire time. Check it out. And you can use your vacation to start exploring the activities you've been discussing, including volunteer opportunities. One of Crys' friends at Saddle Up! has so much vacation accrued that she's taking every Friday off. She's practicing for retirement days as she spends part of her time off volunteering.

Do: The biggest thing we did was to allocate time to experiment and plan and actually do things. I reduced my hours at work to make this happen. For most of the last year of work, I worked half time.

One of the first things Crys and I did with that extra time was to work on a project together. This was very enlightening. While we'd had careers in different industries, it was amazing what we had in common when it came to planning a project. Turns out we both had project management skills. Who knew?

We also found that we liked working together. Wow.

One thing led to another, and soon we began planning the course for a new company called Retirement-U, Inc. And soon after that, I did indeed have something to retire to.

I understand you may not have the luxury of working half time. But don't give up until you've explored some options.

My friend Dave in Alabama is now working four days a week for a total of thirty hours, which is the minimum he can work to keep insurance benefits. This opportunity gives Dave extended time off to work at what the future might bring and feel like.

Are you planning to retire at age 67? You may want to consider postponing your retirement if you can. Put it off in favor of working part-time. You might consider putting off claiming Social Security until age 70. The Social Security delay will mean increased benefit checks later.

If you are in a profession that offers sabbatical, take it. It gives you time to rummage around and see what your life might be like without the demands of work.

My friend John never really had a problem retiring. As the owner of a small business, John had perfect control of when he'd be at work. Everybody knew he would be out on the links every afternoon it was warm enough. When he retired, he only had a few hours of daylight left to schedule.

Another way you could work part-time is to become a consultant. I've had a host of acquaintances over the years retire and then pretty quickly go back to work for the same folks or for others as a consultant.

My wife did that. When she retired, she took a big project with her. She is still working on contract for other folks in the publishing business. Our friend Marcia is contracting now; she goes in to work after exercise two days a week. My other friend John retired from a job with the state and turned around to accept a job keeping books. Another friend Dave now does basically the same IT job three days a week he used to do for five, but he doesn't have to go to meetings!

These options are an invaluable gift in so many ways; you too can get:

Time to rest: Working part-time gives you some time off. You will be surprised at how much better you feel not having to do the job all the time. Working less gives you a new lease on life.

I bet you've known a retiree who has come back to the workplace for a visit. Have you ever wondered why he or she looked so rested? Time off will do that for you, even if it is not full time off.

Time to exercise: I hardly knew I had time off because we converted the bulk of it straight to getting serious about fitness. This in itself has brought a host of benefits, including feeling better and having the energy to do new things. Have you ever noticed that your retired friends actually look better? Cutting your hours gives you room to be more active. You will look better if you convert an inactive life to an active one.

Time to experiment: My wife and I got to find out if we could work together. She said she wanted me for better or for worse. With time off, we got to try being home for lunch too. Turned out we like each other.

Time to invest: With more time, you can find places to volunteer, take a course on your favorite topic, find some new friends and spend time with them, check out the Y, community center, or senior center. You can also take that part-time job you hoped you'd get to try once retired, which doesn't give you time off; but it does answer the question of whether this job is the right step or not.

Time to transition: As a benefit, you let the idea of retirement gain some traction in your life. Until you give it some real time, retirement is only a hope or a promise.

Taking time to sample retirement gives you the opportunity to appreciate what it is about.

Working less also lets you back away from your investment at work. You can begin to let the demands keep their distance. Think of the process as a teeter-totter. When you work for a living you have your feet on the ground and retirement is way over at the other end, up in the sky.

Taking time off means pushing off the ground a little. You can move toward the middle. It gives retirement a level chance with work. And because you're at the balance point, you won't be sliding into either direction until you want.

Plan, try, and do. These are the three steps to preparing for a meaningful retirement. You are allowed to take small steps. In fact I encourage it. If you are the least bit reluctant to try new things, small steps make the trying easier.

For You

The best way I've found to do small steps is to make SMART goals. You can refer again to the list in Appendix C or, for even more details and samples, at the website for this book:

www.retireto.info/goforward/bookresources

Conclusion

Anyone can open doors of more doing. I encourage you to open doors of more *meaning*:

- Seeing the sights is the easy thing to do. Finding *beauty* in them means learning about balance, proportion, viewpoint, and also being engaged with the object.
- Visiting an historic place is the easy thing to do. Finding the *lessons learned* through the experiences of people at that site may very well mean you have to dredge up the heartfelt emotions that were at play or the agonies involved because of the decisions made or actions taken at that place.

Meaning is an investment. You have to engage.

In this book, I hope you have found a starting place for tackling the challenge of reengaging in life in ways that energize you. And I hope you've seen possibilities of reinvesting in activities and people that give you purpose and allow you to give back.

Retirement has brought me a better sense of proportion. I hope I've given you permission to bring more balance into your life too.

- Add play to your day.
- Do something that brings meaning and purpose into your life.
- Integrate exercise into your day.
- Connect with friends often.[81]
- Do something fun or funny each day and laugh a lot.

Consider the following as your daily mantra:

**A little of this... a little of that...
and not too much of any one thing.**

You will find that retiring to play and purpose truly is how to have an amazing time going forward.

---

81 *Retire to Great Friendships* helps you keep the connections plentiful and meaningful.

About Depression

Simply by being retired, you are more vulnerable to depression. Being aware of the factors and potential triggers and being knowledgeable of the symptoms are steps you can take to minimize your risk or to find effective treatment early.

Defining, analyzing, and treating depression are beyond the scope of this book. Besides, I am not trained to do those things. I can share information commonly available about depression as a starting point, but I urge you to seek an expert who can help if you have any questions or are experiencing any of the symptoms associated with depression.

Depression is not a "one-step, visit your pharmacy and you're done" type of malady. Depression can present a large range of symptoms and can be extremely persistent. Depression patients who receive appropriate treatment can usually achieve a successful outcome, but managing or overcoming the illness may take some time.

Untreated depression can lead to risky behaviors such as alcohol or drug addiction. It can cause problems on the job, ruin relationships, and make healing from serious illness difficult.

Depression is not your fault—nor a flaw in your character. That fact is most important to remember! Depression is also not uncommon, as approximately 14 million American adults suffer because of it. A variety of factors can trigger or add to it:

- **Biology.** We still don't know exactly what happens in the brain when people become depressed. But studies show certain parts of the brain don't seem to be working normally. Depression seems to be affected by changes in the levels of certain chemicals in the brain, called neurotransmitters.

- **Genetics.** Researchers know that if depression runs in your family, you have a higher chance of becoming depressed.

- **Gender.** Studies show that women are about twice as likely as men to become depressed. No one's sure why. The hormonal changes women go through at different times of their lives may be a factor.

- **Age.** Older adults are at higher risk of depression, which can be compounded by other factors—living alone and having a lack of social support.

- **Health conditions.** Conditions such as cancer, heart disease, thyroid problems, chronic pain, and many others increase your risk of becoming depressed.

- **Trauma and grief.** Trauma, such as violence or physical or emotional abuse—whether it's early in life or more recent—can trigger depression. Grief after the death of a friend or loved one is in itself a normal emotion, but like all forms of loss it can sometimes lead to depression.

- **Changes and stressful events.** It's not surprising people become depressed under stressful circumstances—such as during a divorce or while caring for a sick relative. Yet even positive changes—like getting married or starting a new job—can sometimes trigger depression.

- **Medications and substances.** Many prescription drugs can cause symptoms of depression. Alcohol or substance abuse is common in depressed people. It often makes their condition worse.[82]

With retirement, several of these factors come into play, including biology, age, change, stressful events, trauma, and grief.

Because retirement is a major transition and often involves loss, you may find yourself depressed to a certain extent somewhat like someone who is grieving the loss of a spouse or family member. Depression is a natural part of the grieving process according to Dr. Elisabeth Kubler-Ross, the Swiss psychiatrist who studied the loss associated with death and dying.[83]

As with any loss, you can expect to experience most, if not all, of the five stages she identified:

- **Denial and isolation**: In an effort to escape an inevitable loss, we try to pretend it's not really happening.

- **Anger**: As the reality of our situation begins to sink in, we lash out in fury and resentment.

- **Bargaining**: Once the anger burns out, we try to negotiate with a higher power or the universe at large for a different outcome.

---

82 "Recognizing and Treating Depression," www.webmd.com/depression.
83 *On Death and Dying*, by Dr. Elisabeth Kubler-Ross, 1969, Simon and Schuster. While Dr. Kubler-Ross studied the loss associated with death and dying, many psychologists attribute similar stages to other major loss transitions.

- **Depression**: When we finally realize we can't avoid or escape the negative results or consequences, we lose hope.
- **Acceptance**: At last, we come to terms with the reality of our situation and handle it realistically and with some grace.

People with depression often:

- Feel sad or anxious
- Have lost interest in usual activities
- Don't feel like they have any energy
- Are tired more than they used to be
- Have gained or lost weight
- Sleep too much or have trouble sleeping
- Can't concentrate
- Cry at surprising times
- Have aches and pains that won't go away
- Feel guilt, worthlessness, and helplessness
- Feel hopeless or pessimistic
- Lose interest in activities or hobbies once pleasurable, including sex

Steps to take[84]

- Talk with a counselor, a friend, or someone in your church.
- Do activities you enjoy. Going back to a favorite childhood activity may boost spirits.[85]
- Eat healthy meals with fruits and vegetables.

---

84 Many of the symptoms of depression and suggestions in this list come from a fact card published by the American College of Physicians Foundation in 2008. Find out more about the organization at http://www.acponline.org. They also recommend the information at www.medlineplus.gov.

85 *The Secret Strength of Depression*, Fourth Edition, by Frederick Flach, M.D., K.C.H.S. and Peter Whybrow, MD. Copyright © 2009 by Hatherleigh Press.

- Make sure other conditions are controlled, particularly diabetes.[86]
- Exercise or walk at least 30 minutes every day.
- Stop smoking; stop drinking alcohol. (If you're having trouble with these, don't wait to see your doctor, see him or her now.)
- Use curiosity, music, and exercise as "toeholds" out of depression.[87]

When symptoms persist, visit your doctor. Here is a question list:

- What can I do to make my depression better?
- What is the name of my depression medication?
- What time of day should I take my medicine? Can I take it with my other pills?
- Does it matter if I take my medicine with or without food?
- What are the side effects of my depression medicine?
- How long should I take my medicines?
- How long will it be before I see results?

---

86 "National Diabetes Fact Sheet, 2011," produced by the National Center for Disease Control and Prevention. Similar notices appear from the National Diabetes Information Clearinghouse (NDIC).
87 "Climbing Out of Depression," by Rhoda Mills Sommer, L.C.S.W., November 28, 2009. http://relationshiprealities.wordpress.com/2009/11/28/climb-ing-out-of-depression/

Tracking Your Income and Expense

To be at peace with your retirement, you need to know whether you're "making it" moneywise or if you need to take some action. Tracking your income and expense is an essential starting point.

Low-Tech Money Tracking

You don't have to have a computer for tracking your money. As a child, my friend Mike received an allowance along with a small notebook. His father's instructions were simple: "Write down everything you spend." Pretty low-tech! As the practice continued, the father asked additional questions:

- Are you happy with where your money went?
- Did you remember to save any money for the new bike you've wanted?

- Do you want to make a contribution to the church?

Mike said the experience was painful: Who wants to track everything? Over the long haul he found the practice very beneficial. Knowing how his money was spent became an important checkpoint in his lifestyle.

All we're concerned about here is learning what Mike learned through the exercise of keeping track of our money. We're doing it for the same reasons too.

- Are you happy with where your money is going?
- Are you saving?
- Are you giving back to help others?

If you only write a few checks, the notebook may suffice. Most of us write some checks, have some bills paid automatically, and use credit or debit cards so we don't have to carry cash. Keeping up can quickly get complicated, and having the discipline to track everything manually may be a problem. If you learn to put credit card receipts in the same place every time, you can circle back and write the information in the notebook later.

Then you will need to convert your list of payments into a summary of expenses. To figure out how much you spent on food, for example, you have to go back through the list and add up the appropriate items. Repeat the process for medical expenses, eating out, utilities, and so on.

You can more easily categorize expenses if you do it each time you spend something. Start by turning your small notebook sideways. Make some columns and add headings. It will look like this:

Date	Vendor	Check	Food	Rx	Dr	H₂O	Car
6/15	Grocer	1236	72.46				
6/15	Gas	1237					42.16

Here I've made things a little easier on myself by drawing some lines. Because I have limited space, I'm using abbreviations such as H_2O (the chemical symbol for water) as a shortcut for utilities and R_x as a shortcut for drugs. If portability is not an issue, you can make recording easier on yourself by buying some ledger sheets or a ledger book at your stationery supply store.

Such a list can also benefit tax preparation. Who wants to go back through a drawer of receipts to find deductible items? You can minimize problems finding details at tax time by putting a checkmark on all the tax-related items.

High-Tech Money Tracking

When you use a computer, you have a wide variety of options available. Basically, you need to decide a few things and then shop the software options. Here is a list of options:

- Does the software print checks? Do you even want that feature?
- What about automatic transfers or electronic bill paying?
- Does the software automatically categorize and summarize expenses?

- How does the computer find out about your checks or credit card payments?

The following discussion generally divides the software options into two large categories: after-the-fact options and before-the-fact options. If you want to continue writing checks by hand or use credit cards as the primary vehicle to pay expenses, an after-the-fact option may be more appropriate as you won't have to change how you do things. A before-the-fact option lets you print checks using the computer.

After-the-fact solutions

Spreadsheet: You can use Excel (Windows or Mac), Numbers (Mac), or Google Docs (Spreadsheet) on the web. Any of these will let you enter your check and credit card details in a manner very similar to the manual chart shown above. The program will automatically total columns if you wish and summarize things by month, quarter, or year. Generally, these are relatively inexpensive options.

Using a spreadsheet is what I call an after-the-fact, manual accounting solution: you enter details *after* the checks have been written or charges have been made. The system will not print the checks or transfer funds; it knows nothing about the checks you've written unless you tell it.

Automatic Software: Mint (From Mint.com) is another after-the fact solution, but it is an automatic instead of manual system. Once you tell Mint where your bank account(s) and/ or credit card(s) are, it will retrieve new transactions and summarize the data. You do not have to enter checks or charges, and you do not have to assign each check or charge to a category. The program does these for you.

Mint can help you set goals about how you spend your money or, if needed, help you take corrective action.

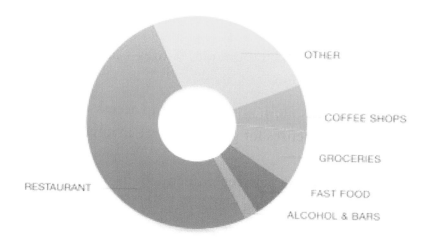

(Based on this summary, I may want to spend a smaller portion of my money eating out!)

Because Mint is a web-based program, desktop or laptop access to the Internet is essential. Apps are available for some phones and tablets as well. I understand Mint's security to be good. The product does have some limits as to which banks it can link to.

I personally remain a loyal and happy user of QuickBooks, a product of Intuit, the company that also makes Mint. Intuit has been in the accounting software business for a long time, so I trust their ability to get the accounting and security details right.

Several other players in the automatic money-tracking game include:

- MoneyDesktop
- Moneytrackin'
- Buxfer
- Mvelopes
- MySpendingPlan

- Outright
- Xero

These programs each have unique features—shop carefully with your needs in mind:

- Allowing a team or family member to access account
- Managing expenses for groups you are involved with
- Budgeting
- Making spending plan recommendations
- Recommending saving plans
- Providing financial advice
- Facilitating envelope budgeting
- Allowing data access via phone, tablet, and computer

Before-the-fact accounting solutions

Another category of accounting software lets you enter check details and then print the checks; you are doing the work *before* the check is produced. This type of product also lets you enter credit card details (after the fact), reconcile bank and credit card accounts, and usually lets you enter details about vendors.

These programs are generally designed for desktop or laptop use and often can be modified to include additional features like invoicing, general ledger, and so on. These products are a lot less expensive than full-blown, large capacity, multiuser software packages for large companies for tracking payroll, inventory, bill-of-materials (and on and on), but they are more expensive than the after-the-fact software listed earlier.

You have choices among the growing numbers of players in this market, as well:

Product	Mac	Windows
QuickBooks	✓	✓
Quicken	✓	✓
MoneyWorks	✓	✓
iBank 4	✓	

You can find many titles by searching on "personal finance software" in your web search engine of choice. You will also get reviews. If you are a Mac hound, look up reviews in *Mac Life* or *MacMagazine*. *PC World* or *PC Magazine* provides good information for Windows users.

Tax returns

If you have an accountant, you may wish to follow his or her lead. Some accounting programs, particularly in the desktop/laptop variety can exchange data with your accountant. This exchange can minimize some work for you at tax preparation time.

More on SMART goals

SMART goals are just plain smart! They are simple, yet great tools for helping you move from thinking about to doing!

SMART goal components

Start with **Specific** objectives. "I will live a life of purpose" is a laudable goal, but not a specific objective. "I will volunteer at the homeless shelter" is specific.

The specific objective in a SMART goal has to be **Measurable**. Putting a measurement to an objective helps you avoid vague or too-broad goals that cannot be attained. If you can measure key elements, the goal is much more likely to be specific.

On the other hand, "I will make 5,000 cookies" may be specific and measurable, but that goal may be nearly unattainable. You can overdo. Watch that the goals you write are **<u>A</u>ttainable**.

<u>R</u>elevant is also important. You have to pick things that will make sense in context.

> *This week I will review the literature that I've collected about running shoes.*

This example shows the beginning of an excellent SMART goal. But is it relevant to the task at hand? Your SMART goals must maintain the focus on the achievements you envision. Writing those why or benefit statements will be helpful here, as well.

Finally, your SMART goal should be **<u>T</u>ime-bound**. Setting deadlines is important for two reasons: motivation and focus. If I know I'm on a short leash, I'm less likely to wander around chasing the wrong thing.

SMART goal examples

#1 – I want to be sure to not isolate myself.

- I will go to the Wednesday night dinner program at church to see who else participates. I'll call Monday morning to reserve a slot.
- I'm going to check out the bridge club at the Y. I understand they meet weekly. Next week I'll know whether or not to look elsewhere for a good card game.
- The slow-riders bicycle club has been after me to join. I will go ride with them Saturday morning. Note to self: Look up the time tomorrow!

#2 – I need more structure to my time.

- I will get up for breakfast five days this week.
- Tomorrow I'm calling the Y and getting a class schedule for water aerobics. I want to find morning classes.
- By Sunday evening I will review my week to make sure I have a plan for at least one thing each day that gets me moving in a positive direction.

#3 – I need a new way to talk about myself. Now that I'm not working, what's my identity?

- I'm going to make notes about a new elevator spiel. By next week I will write some retirement experiences that capture what I've been doing.
- Tomorrow I'm taking my wife for a surprise lunch. I will ask her what my life looks like from the outside looking in.
- John and I are playing pool next Thursday. I'll ask him what he tells people when they ask, "What do you do?"

#4 – Take a trip! Just the ticket.

- Isn't it time we got to see our friends in Pennsylvania again? I'm going to give them a call this week and see what they're up to in June.
- I don't remember the last time I took Crys on an anniversary trip. I wonder what surprise I can dig up for her this year. Sunday afternoon I'll do a web search on bed and breakfasts in Indiana. We haven't been up that way in a while.
- Oh. We're taking our grandson to a Road Scholar trip next month. I need to check a map and see what inter-

esting things there are to see on the way. It'd be good to have that done Friday so Crys and I can talk about it over the weekend.

#5 – I can be a volunteer!

- I used to love horses. I'm going to check the Internet to find some type of volunteer activity around horses. I want to get back in.
- My friend John ushers people at the symphony to their seats. I'd like to do something like that. I'll call tomorrow and see how to go about it.
- I don't know where to volunteer. I'm sure some website will get me in touch with volunteer activities around here. I'm going to look that up. By next Monday I want to start making calls.

I encourage you to look up the material on the Retire-To website resource page. You will find even more samples of goals and also be able to print them, which may give you a head start for setting ones of you own. See these materials at:

www.retireto.info/goforward/bookresources/

Other Books by Ed Zinkiewicz

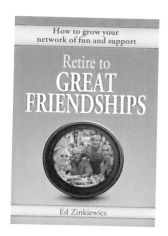

Retire to Great Friendships
How to grow your network of fun and support

Retire to a Better You
How to be *able* for the rest of your life

**Find more details about these
and other resources at**

Retire-To.com

CPSIA information can be obtained at www.ICGtesting.com
Printed in the USA
LVOW01s0741121113

360971LV00003B/8/P

9 780988 662223